THE BOOKSHOP THAT
FLOATED AWAY

One day, a very strange business plan landed on the desk of a pinstriped bank manager. It included pictures of Cleopatra's barge and Ratty and Mole in their rowing boat — and petitioned for a loan to purchase a narrowboat plus a small hoard of books. Unsuprisingly, the application was rejected: undaunted, Sarah still succeeded in realising her dream of creating a floating bookshop. Captaining The Book Barge on a six-month tour of Britain's waterways, she is thrown into the deep end of waterborne literature retail: learning the intricacies of lock operation; bartering paperbacks for accommodation, bathroom facilities and cake; and rescuing stranded pigeons named Nelson . . .

SPECIAL MESSAGE TO READERS

THE ULVERSCROFT FOUNDATION
(registered UK charity number 264873)
was established in 1972 to provide funds for research, diagnosis and treatment of eye diseases.
Examples of major projects funded by the Ulverscroft Foundation are:-

- The Children's Eye Unit at Moorfields Eye Hospital, London
- The Ulverscroft Children's Eye Unit at Great Ormond Street Hospital for Sick Children
- Funding research into eye diseases and treatment at the Department of Ophthalmology, University of Leicester
- The Ulverscroft Vision Research Group, Institute of Child Health
- Twin operating theatres at the Western Ophthalmic Hospital, London
- The Chair of Ophthalmology at the Royal Australian College of Ophthalmologists

You can help further the work of the Foundation by making a donation or leaving a legacy. Every contribution is gratefully received. If you would like to help support the Foundation or require further information, please contact:

THE ULVERSCROFT FOUNDATION
**The Green, Bradgate Road, Anstey
Leicester LE7 7FU, England
Tel: (0116) 236 4325**

website: oft.com

46 841 268 7

A former journalist, Sarah Henshaw is now the proud owner of The Book Barge, which is currently in business somewhere on the water in rural Staffordshire.

Visit her website at:
www.thebookbarge.com

SARAH HENSHAW

◆

THE
BOOKSHOP THAT
FLOATED AWAY

Complete and Unabridged

ULVERSCROFT
Leicester

First published in Great Britain in 2014 by
Constable
an imprint of
Constable & Robinson Ltd, London

First Large Print Edition
published 2015
by arrangement with
Constable & Robinson Ltd, London

A catalogue record for this book is available
from the British Library.

ISBN 978–1–4448–2507–7

Published by
F. A. Thorpe (Publishing)
Anstey, Leicestershire

Set by Words & Graphics Ltd.
Anstey, Leicestershire
Printed and bound in Great Britain by
T. J. International Ltd., Padstow, Cornwall

This book is printed on acid-free paper

For Stu. And for my parents.

'I have no business but with myself.'
Michel de Montaigne

Introduction

Almost daily, customers ask why I have a bookshop on a boat. Sometimes their tone of voice suggests genuine interest. Usually it is to precede a pun they actually believe to be original — about it being a 'novel' idea. Or one 'hull' of an idea. Or, when the American tourists are in, a 'swell' idea. Once it was asked with an inflection tending towards hysteria as the woman, peering from a far window, shrieked: 'We're actually on water! Maggie, you didn't tell me this was a real boat! You, at the desk, WHY IS THIS SHOP AFLOAT?' She then paused, pulled a paperback to her chest as if to shield against some kind of half-understood canal alchemy, before reconsidering: 'But is it afloat? I just realised, this is all probably some 3D illusion.' More thought. 'On stilts.'

And so I launch into a well-rehearsed and quite truthful spiel about the relative cost-effectiveness of a floating premises as opposed to one on the high street, or how the quirkiness attracts greater footfall, the advantages of being able to move on when business is slack and, on Friday afternoons when a couple of glasses of cheap wine have unspooled an embarrassing romantic readiness, I say that books and boats just go together. 'Adventure!' I cry. 'Escape!' I trill. And then straight into a chronology of craft-inspired literature, beginning with *The Life and Strange Surprising Adventures of Robinson Crusoe, Of York, Mariner: Who lived Eight-and-Twenty Years, all alone in an uninhabited Island on the Coast of America, near the Mouth of the Great River of Oronoque; Having been cast on Shore by Shipwreck, wherein all the Men perished but himself. With an Account how he was at last as strangely deliver'd by Pyrates.* 'For that was Defoe's considerably longer original title,' I slur, winking knowledgeably. I am nothing if not didactic on £4.99 Co-op Sauvignon Blanc from a plastic cup.

The Book Barge took shape in 2009. My boyfriend and I petitioned several banks for loans to buy the boat. They all saw the same supporting document, which was, I can now clearly appreciate, a nonsense. It was presented as a book (my idea). It included a title page with the pun-heavy, poorly written tagline: 'The locks could not imprison her. The waterways could not drown her spirit. She defied canal convention to become . . . THE BOOK BARGE.' I am squirming. Weirdly, at the time, I thought this was a kooky approach to business financing that would win over even the most hardened, calculator-for-a-heart manager. I now realise I was being a tit. There were fictional endorsements: 'Gripping! A masterpiece of business prose' — *Finance Digest*. 'You can bank on this having a happy ending' — *The Investor Times*. Inside, the 'chapters' had dumb-ass names like 'An Interesting Proposal', 'A Fortuitous Partnership' (to describe Stu's and my faux business credentials) and 'A Great Number of Numbers', which presented highly optimistic sales forecasts as an Excel spreadsheet, sandwiched between pictures of Cleopatra's barge and Ratty and Mole gesticulating on a blue wooden rowing boat. An interesting proposal? It was frankly indecent. Our loan application was turned down firmly — and frequently — and we were forced to borrow from family instead.

When we first opened, it seemed like the gamble would pay off; business was brisk and the events the shop hosted were well attended. But the industry was changing, and it was changing fast. A year later, consumer sales of ebooks and downloads already accounted for 11 per cent of the British book market (up from 2 per cent when The Book Barge launched). Meanwhile, national headlines were still dominated by statistics warning of Britain's worst double-dip recession in fifty years. Suddenly browsers were borrowing pencils to scribble down ISBNs to purchase later, for less, online. The question everyone asked was now slightly different: not, 'Why do you have a bookshop on a boat?' but 'Why do you have a bookshop at all?'

Frustrated and struggling financially, I set off in May 2011 on a six-month journey to raise awareness, not just of my plight, but of the uncertain future facing all high-street bookstores. It turned out to be transformative in a more wonderful way than I imagined. There's a line in Emma Smith's canalling memoir, *Maidens' Trip*, claiming the waterways offered her a life that, for once, lived up to all her expectations, and that's what happened here too. More than that, I felt complete confidence and satisfaction in what I was doing. It made me indescribably happy.

This was almost entirely down to the people who bought, swapped or donated books, the ones who emailed a complete stranger to say nice things about the venture, the ones who refrained from swearing when I collided into their houseboats, the ones who made cups of tea, the ones who made Victoria sponge cakes, the ones who enlisted as 'crew' to bypass archaic Bristol trading laws, the ones who hauled a boat from a lock in Yorkshire when I flooded it, the woman who suggested a book bus might be easier, and the three sheep who jumped over a drystone wall to see what all the fuss was about when I yelled hysterically back at her that she should mind her own business. Staying afloat, I discovered, was only half the story.

PART ONE

1

WATER (part i)

There are two types of skinny dippers in this world: those who do it because the idea of being naked in water is titillating and/or liberating. And those who misguidedly believe that no one can see them naked *because* they are in water. I suspect there are only a handful of people in the latter category. Growing up in South Africa, my sister and I were two of these.

Durban, 1990. We swim most afternoons after school at the hospital where our father works. It's invariably empty, but at 4 p.m. a man called Mr Priggy comes through the gate with a bucket of chlorine powder and empties this around us. At weekends our whole family comes, and the neighbouring family too, and so there are eleven of us in or around the water. The parents usually recline on loungers in the shade. Us children dive or belly flop or swim lengths underwater or play a game called Marco Polo, which is an aquatic version of blind man's bluff. I don't know why it is called Marco Polo because, as far as

3

I'm aware, Marco Polo wasn't blind. From pictures I've seen, nor does he look like the kind of guy given to the frivolity of *pretending* to be blind, especially in pools. When I'm playing it, I don't much think about the origins of Marco Polo. I'm shouting loud refrains of 'Polo!' whenever the unseeing 'It' tries to gauge our whereabouts with a questioning 'Marco?'. I'm swallowing lots of water too. This game is my favourite. I don't even mind being 'It'. All I know of Marco Polo is that he was an explorer, and blindly voyaging into the unknown, like him, seems not such a bad way to spend an afternoon.

My sister and I love being in the water. We stay in after everyone else has towelled off and turned into each other to chat and eat thick cheese sandwiches. This is when my sister suggests we take off our swimming costumes. 'No one will know because no one can see under water.' We have an identical style of swimming costume. Our mother made them for us. They have a scooped back, tanning matching parabolas on us. Above the crack of our bums is a bow. Hers is pink. Mine is blue. We take them off and put them on the hot, tiled side of the pool where they look like the rain-ruined petals of an exotic flower. We are naked and giggling. Following her logic, I put my whole head under water so no one can see me at all. It's a shame that no one can see us, I think, because when we pull the water with our arms and legs we must look like little birds against a blue sky.

Years pass. We grow up, school, study, get jobs, move away. I open a bookshop on a canal boat near the brewing town and Marmite metropolis of Burton-on-Trent, England. It doesn't sell many books. The water around it is not like the water we grew up with in the pool. It is dark and brown. I could take off my clothes in it and no one would know I was naked, but I would not look like a bird. Across the marina is a dual carriageway and an Argos warehouse. I look out of the window at them and at the water. It is not like any water I know. It doesn't run towards me like a dog, pawing my shoulders, as the waves do on a beach. It doesn't cry in my hair like rain. Mostly it just lies there, unsharing except for a dead trout it squeezes between the hull of the boat and the promenade one week in the summer.

If this was a mean trick, it goes one better that winter. For two weeks after Christmas it freezes over. When I look out of the window now there are fissures that look like small, bare trees lightly foresting the lake. Mostly they're around the sides of the boats — my boat too — hedging us neatly in. I can't see the water through the ice and stop worrying about it. I have lots of bills unpaid in the red filing cabinet by my desk to divert my attention instead. It's been a long time since I took any money from the business.

As it gets warmer and the ice starts to waste away there's a surprise on the boat. When I open up at 10 a.m. I can hear things are different because the boat is gurgling like a bad lung. The inside is flooded and I'm puzzled to see how clear the water is. For a moment it looks like a long pool in there. Bookshelves are toothed unevenly along its length and those on the bottom are swollen now and my heart aches at all the money gone into them. I turn off the water pressure and find where the pipe has burst, which is in a cupboard full of more wet books. Their pages are limp and thin. All the words on them are confused by the words you can see behind. The water has crowded them like frightened herd animals. I phone my boyfriend, Stu, and we try to empty some water with buckets and a wet vac. If the ice was thinner maybe we'd be able to steer the boat across to the pump at the boatyard and have it all out in minutes. But we're still there in the evening and my father goes Victor Frankenstein in his garage to produce something that hoses it out a little faster, powered by his orange electric drill.

When we're finished it's not so bad and I can open up a few days later. I feel like the boat has had enough of this marina though — and I have too. I press my nose against the condensation on the window to form dot-to-dot pictures while I wait for customers. It's a rush to complete them with my index finger before drips ruin the fragile images and I'm glad no one can see me.

2

WATER (part ii)

At around this time, I start searching for wooden rowing boats on eBay. Stu keeps telling me we can't afford one, but I've seen a young couple turn up at the marina pub on one and I want that for ourselves. They had laughed so hard trying to get off their boat and onto the promenade. The boat had rocked and their legs shook as if they were scurvy-weakened from a long, long journey in it together. When they were inside the pub I hurried out to look at their boat with the oars crossed in a kiss.

I find one eventually for £200 and buy it. Its outer shell is painted a bruised red but inside is just plain yacht-varnished wood. Because the narrow boat's name is Joseph, I call the little one Josephine and it stays upside down on the roof of the shop. Stu is furious. He's working two jobs at the time to pay our bills and when he comes home from his second shift — late, often at midnight — I'm miserable with guilt and twice as angry back at him. I'm working seven days a week in the bookshop but it counts for nothing financially. I remember how my sister and I used to predict each other's romantic future when we were little. I always told her exactly what she wanted to hear — that she would marry a farmer or a dog handler or a horse whisperer and he'd buy her new pets every birthday and have strong forearms. But she never returned the fantasy for me. I wanted to live in sin and fingerless gloves in a cold garret. She pointed out that I have bad circulation in my fingers and insisted my wedded fate was with a rich businessman in a large, double-glazed house. As a concession to my vehement complaints, she granted I could have an affair with the gardener. Only fifteen years on and completely broke does her forecast seem suddenly more reasonable.

In between my arguments with Stu there's this thing called boredom. I suppose it's always been around, haunting wet summer holidays and long car journeys. When it turns up on the boat one morning I choose not to acknowledge it. I'm finding this a useful tool to deal with most things that come down those steps. But it stays longer each time, leafing through the mounting piles of unsold books, making beautiful origami swans from the invoices stuffed in drawers. It doesn't do any of the things that annoy me in other customers, but I find its lurking presence uncomfortable. I won't speak. I turn the radio volume up and angle the computer screen out of its puzzled sightline.

One day a man walks into the bookshop to order I-Spy books for his son. He doesn't live around here but he likes boats and was curious about the shop. He returns a few weeks later to pick the books up and stays longer this time to talk. I like hearing him speak, especially when he's talking about sailing. He brings me some books about boats and shows me photos online of the Scandinavian sloop he's just bought in America. 'I'd like to cross the Atlantic in that,' I say. 'Why not?' he replies, 'September's a good time.' So I spend even more money on sailing gear and a life jacket and buying a big Imray chart mapping a September Atlantic crossing. I dream of big waves pounding out all the mistakes I've made with the bookshop and with Stu. I imagine coming back a different person, someone we will both like more.

A month before I'm due to leave, I move out of the flat I share with Stu and back in with my parents. I want Stu to tell me to stay, but we're both out of confidence. I get some clothes and he helps me put them in a big black bin liner and takes it to the car. The summer, which I hadn't noticed happen, is also hastily packing her things. There's a mess of trampled petal by the bottom step of the front door. How did a season escape us that year? I don't know it's over until I'm driving away. I see Stu standing, smile set, setting with the heavy sun in the rearview mirror.

★ ★ ★

The man with the boat gives me sailing lessons on Windermere. Even though I don't know exactly what I'm doing, he lets me take the wheel and guess with the sails while he goes downstairs and makes calls on his mobile phone. I like these moments and the lake. The sky greys us both and gets me thinking of a book I'm reading about boredom. It explains that boredom is a force, that it moves us and compels us to do things. Out there on the lake, boredom feels like the wind, and I jibe with it. I jump in the water with no clothes and feel happy that I don't need to battle boredom any longer. I pull it close to me with the cold water. When I look up and see the man with the boat watching me, I am conscious of how wrong my sister was about water. It doesn't cloak me. With my head under and my hair in its fingers it bares everything.

In the car on the way back, the man tells me about his job. He's a businessman. As always, I like hearing him speak. I look straight out of the front window at the grey motorway and suddenly know that I won't cross the Atlantic on his boat and that it doesn't matter. I start planning another journey — just me and my books and my canal boat. I feel like I have to do something because otherwise I'm just wondering about Stu and getting angry that people aren't buying books. Chekhov says of inspiration that if you look at anything long enough, say just that wall in front of you, it will come out of that wall. I have no reason to distrust him. I like his short stories more than any others.

3

GARDEN

My plans for the trip are vague. I figure you can't be too sure when the gardener's going to turn up in your life story so I'm taking no chances. I concentrate mainly on furnishing the roof of the boat with a fifty-foot length of fake turf. There are a few potted plants up there too, which my mother buys, and an orange flower from my friend Ali. These all die in the first few weeks, mainly because I forget to water them. I leave them up there anyway — neglected vegetation is just as likely to get a green-fingered lover's blood pounding as blooming, pruned stuff, I reckon.

Stu gives me a golden pot to grow sunflowers in. When we started dating ten years earlier he wrote out the lyrics to Paul Weller's *Sunflower* on an old cassette tape. He had replaced the tape ribbon with white ribbon and winding it on with a little finger revealed the whole song biro'd across. I used to sit on my bedroom floor rolling through it a lot. I liked the line about a wheat field for hair. Now, when he gives me the pot for the sunflowers, I start crying.

I've decided the trip will be six months long, beginning in May. Ostensibly it's a mission to save my shop, The Book Barge. If I leave it where and how it is, it'll close in a much shorter length of time. If I'm honest, I suspect it'll close anyway. I'm borrowing so much money from family and Stu and the bank already to keep it going. But if it closes, I don't want it to be in front of the people who keep coming in and drinking the free tea and telling me it's such a shame people aren't buying enough books — and then leaving without buying any books.

Mostly, though, I want to be alone. Alone for a whole summer — *The Solitary Summer* — as a book of the same name describes another woman demanding some 100 years earlier. Elizabeth von Arnim was the pen name of Mary Annette Beauchamp, a British novelist who, in 1891, married a Prussian aristocrat. She later unflatteringly referred to him as the 'Man of Wrath'. It was to escape him and their brood of children that one evening she hit upon the idea of spending six months in solitude — or as close to it as she could get without entirely evading parental/spousal duties. Only in such a prolonged period of quiet contemplation, she thought,

14

could she get to 'the very dregs of life', reflect on her mistakes, bask in idleness, watch nature unfold and 'be perpetually happy, because there will be no one to worry me'.

The book it spawned is much more than a pretty sort of genteel feminist protest. It's about quietly discovering a sense of self and working out how best to engage with life. I want both of those things. Unfortunately, as yet I don't quite have the small fortune and vast family estate in Nassenheide, Pomerania to accommodate this half-year grapple with philosophy. But I have a boat and modest hoard of books. Something can be made of that.

In fact, the solution is in that very book. Von Arnim adored reading. 'What a blessing it is to love books,' she wrote. 'Everybody must love something, and I know of no objects of love that give such substantial and unfailing returns as books.' Clearly she wasn't talking in a business sense. Book *selling* is ruining me. But 'return' in a less strictly financial — but still economic — sense? That could be done. I figure bartering stock instead for the food and facilities I need on the trip makes both romantic and pragmatic sense. In fact, it resonates more deeply than that. For the last two years I've been bemoaning the unfair playing field independent booksellers compete on against online and supermarket retailers, who can afford to massively discount their prices to lure in cost-conscious customers. An experiment like this could be a useful corrective to the easy acceptance that value for money has just one currency. Consumers have come to expect discounts. In fact, most feel positively cheated if a price tag hasn't been visibly slashed. By offering goods without any money at all exchanging hands, The Book Barge could become an attractive proposition to buyers who are open-minded enough to appreciate the value of a noncapitalist organisation. And I could benefit from a spare sofa every now and then.

At the very least, encouraging readers to understand a book's value as an item equivalent to, for example, a pub meal rather than a '3-for-2' chain store marketing reduction can only be a good thing. Maybe, just maybe, it can even make a reader reconsider where and how they buy their books.

In case customers don't play game, I try to address some of my more basic needs before leaving. Mainly, I'm concerned with where to wee and where to wash. That the boat catered for both when it was first bought is a source of brief anguish. The original cassette toilet and shower still sit in my parents' garage but the time and cost of retro-fitting them makes me insist there must be other, easier ways.

So I buy a portable camping shower on the internet, and then five more just in case they're as badly manufactured as their price tag suggests. I also buy a paddling pool to act as a basin for all the showers. I don't want any more water damage to the stock. The one I choose is pretty babyish and based on a kids' TV show called *In The Night Garden*. I've never watched the show, so the detachable 'Upsy Daisy inflatable character feature' is a bit lost on me and I bin it. However, it has a natty hosepipe feature so that water can spray out and the providence of the show's name doesn't escape me either. Gardener's going to love these little touches. The weeing problem demands more time and thought.

4

FUD

I discover that what I'm after is something called a FUD — a Female Urinary Device — which will funnel pee into a bottle. There are also things called STP devices (Stand-To-Pee), which are the same, I think. These acronyms are for real. There's a Wikipedia page with a concise breakdown of different brands, like the WhizBiz and the P-Mate and the SheWee and the GoGirl (tagline: 'Don't take life sitting down'). In France, there's one called a Urinelle, which I start calling mine in a throaty Gallic accent, even though it's just a generic camping shop one. I also have a spare 'feminine attachment' that came with the plastic portable urinal (a bottle) I bought off Amazon. I usually have more qualms about using Amazon, but when it comes to shopping for liquid excretory vessels, I find it difficult to take a moral high ground.

I learn some pretty fascinating stuff on that Wikipedia page, for example that some FUDs are NATO-approved and supplied to military personnel, and also that it's possible to achieve a perfectly good STP aim without the aid of these handheld devices. In fact, 'this was the norm in much earlier times'. I'm starting to feel in thrall to history. I've never really viewed the narrow boat in any other context than as a quirky shop space, but now I'm watching canal documentaries and reading up on their working-boat past, including some great 1940s memoirs about women who formed three-girl crews to help the war effort. They used buckets for their 'business'; I am interested to compare.

Although my FUD should be an empowering convenience, I worry I won't have much chance to use it. Despite having had the boat for nearly three years now, I've never deemed it necessary to find out how it works or steers. As such, I'm not entirely sure how I'll stop it when I do need a wee. Holding in wee indefinitely scares me a little. I come from a medical family and they confirm it's probably not healthy. In the days leading up to departure I worry I'll suffer the same fate that befell Peter the Great, whom I learned about during A-Level history. Peter the Great was the single best thing I took from school. I had a teacher called Mr Bowman who lent me the Lindsey Hughes biography so I could find out even more facts at home. In class, Mr

Bowman would tell us about the Boyars being forced to cut off their beards and how the Great Northern War happened. He made sure we all spelt 'naval' correctly in our essays. But after a double lesson on Thursdays, I would go home and read about the fiercest of all Peter's passions — his love of boats and the sea.

It made sense to me in land-locked Staffordshire that Peter the Great could also grow up lusting for ocean, despite the fact he didn't encounter open sea until he was twenty-one. Like the canal-veined Midlands, his Russia relied on the inland waterways instead and the small craft that plied these lazy rivers. As a child he played toy boats and collected nauticalia. Maybe he woke up some nights in his palace bed briefly happier than he had ever known, because he thought the white shroud of his sheet was sail cloth, it was so cold against his skin. One day he found an old English sailing dinghy in the outbuilding of a country estate. He said this was the boat that made him master of Europe. He called it the grandfather of the Russian fleet.

But when I remember Peter the Great and his boats, I also can't help recalling the weird way he was killed by his own urine. Over the years, my memory has confused and entwined the two so that I'm surprised, writing this now, to have Lindsay Hughes tell me he died in bed — and not from his bladder spontaneously exploding on a frigate in the Finnish Gulf. In fact, his urinary tract problems were drawn out over two years. In the summer of 1724, he had four pounds of blocked yellow stuff released by a team of doctors. He suffered from a condition called uremia. As well as being painful, it can sometimes lead to a complication called uremic frost. It's when the urea comes out of your face and white powders all over your wan cheeks and sunken eyes and salt-dried lips. Ivan Nikitich Nikitin, the Russian painter who captured Peter's portrait on his death in 1725, sensitively omitted this detail. You'd never know the Tsar had crusty piddle on his distinguished brow, like a snow-man recently shoved down a U-bend. Nikitin shades him avocado instead. An autopsy later revealed his bladder was infected with gangrene.

I try not to think about any of this and enjoy my last few days on dry land making the most of regular, seated flushes and once, in the shower, venturing an upright tinkle without props. Old school. When I do set off, on the morning of 3rd May, I make light of my first desperate situation by interrupting a text conversation with the short, exclamatory: 'Need WC! FUD! LOL! BRB after STP. ALOL! xoxoxo'[1]

---

[1] translates as: 'Need loo! I have a handy Female Urinary Device to help with that! Laughing out loud, but that's not a good idea on a full bladder. Be right back after standing to pee into a Lucozade bottle and examining myself for pissy frostbite. *Actually* laughing out loud! (Actually crying inside).'

5

TED

Apart from my parents, one other person waves me off. His name is Ted and I've known him the whole time I've been moored at the marina. Ted lives on a little plastic cruising boat on the jetty across the water from my spot on the promenade. Like me, when Ted looks out of the window, he can see the dual carriageway and the Argos warehouse. Something I don't know until much later is that Ted's boat is slowly sinking and will take him with it. Every day he bails out the brown water, and all the while his chest complains and leaks air noisily. He tries to catch it in his mouth on the way out but it slithers off like lots of tiny silver fish.

Ted smells really bad because he wears the same blue-and-red checked flannel shirt every day. When I see him out of the window walking towards my boat with his mouth snatching I'll always rush to meet him before he can come in the shop and make it smell bad too. If there are customers on the boat I don't have to do this because Ted doesn't like them and won't come in. Once, on a Thursday afternoon when there were mums and toddlers aboard and I was reading them picture books, he pressed a big piece of cow offal against the window at us. He stayed like that, grinning, with the meat in his hand smudging blood behind the glass and the clear plastic of its bag. When I went outside because the mums and toddlers were getting upset at him, he started telling me about the curry he was going to make with it, because he loved talking about cooking. He showed off the meat again like a prize.

The first thing Ted ever told me was that he'd once been arrested for hanging his girl-friend's knickers up a church steeple in London. My mouth fell open and closed like his. She'd been running around with another man and when Ted found out, he took her drawer of drawers up the nearest tower in retaliation. Soon there was a blue tinselling of police lights around the base of the church but Ted kept climbing higher. He must've looked like King Kong, he said. Other people started gathering to watch. When they looked up at him through the peak of their hands and the early-morning sun they could see the bunting of thongs and a pair of sheer tights tied to the line around his waist. He wore a bra over his head but every few minutes it fell forward

24

onto his eyes and stalled his progress. He had to lean into a recess and let go with his left hand and reposition the cups back on his head and pull the straps tight around his chin again. After this had happened a few times, a schoolboy who was watching on the opposite side of the road started a chorus of spidermaninnit spidermaninnit spidermaninnit spidermaninnit spidermaninnit spidermaninnit spidermaninnit.

When Ted got to the top he could hardly breathe. He held his girlfriend's knickers in a fist to pump the air and then let them go. The line didn't fall much, snagged, and stayed — all those tiny G-stringed ensigns of his rage. The crowd tunnelled its breath collectively as Ted fell forward and searched for air with his hands. Police climbed up the fire stairs to reach him. His chest drummed them on. 'They had inflatables waiting at the bottom because everyone thought I would fall,' he said. 'But all they caught was a single pair of her pants, and a boy ran over and grabbed them and held them up like a big fish for everyone to see.'

When Ted told the story, his eyes were laughing but the tattoo on his chest was buzzing up and down louder than the wasp on the windowsill in the boat. I took what he said and grafted my own tale to tell friends. I flesh it each time with higher towers, more lingerie. The peril of his asthma grows. I tell it without any audience too. Over the next few months, alone on the boat, I play it over and over in my head. Ted said that sometimes, when things aren't fair, a person needs to protest and that they should do it any which way they want to.

6

DIGRESSION

I am hopeful of reaching Fradley Junction before autumn, which I do that same morning. This is a great surprise. Less of one to my father, who has come with me until lunch, worked all the locks, and has a better grasp of geography. After this small milestone (a voyage of five, to be precise) I feel brave enough to describe an ambiguous figure of eight in the air with my finger to the first customer who asks where the next six months will take me. This turns out to be a woman called Helen Tidy.

Helen and her husband, Andrew, are waterways gurus. Their boat, Wand'ring Bark, accommodates her hedgerow jam business and inspires his canal-boating blog. It also carries a name taken from the only Shakespeare sonnet I know off by heart — and that purely because Greg Wise swooningly recited it to Kate Winslet in *Sense and Sensibility* (The Movie I Juvenilely Watched Too Many Times). It's about the constancy of true love. More than that — it describes how love can help steer your course through life.

I have *a lot* of love for that first customer. She swaps me a home-baked Wild Flower Syrup Cake and graciously overlooks my narrow boating naïveté (I'm on the wrong canal, having overshot the turning to Birmingham). As such, I'm open to her direction. When she reveals she's on her way to Stratford-upon-Avon, I resolve to make it my first port of call too. That there are sixty-five locks standing in my way, I care little. I have still not done one on my own. I put the boat in reverse, discover steering is impossible backwards, slam into a British Waterways tug and utter another two immortal words lifted directly from Sonnet 116: 'O no!'

★ ★ ★

One problem with this story is that there are not enough characters like Helen or Ted in it. Characters that crop up reliably, I mean, that a reader can get to know. I see Helen or her husband three more times. Ted appears again near the end, where he dies. That's not a spoiler by the way. When I told you this in the last chapter, that was the spoiler. This story is about a journey where I swap books for food or a bathroom or a bed. As such, it's a series of very short, quite intense relationships with people I never ever get back together with. Much like a very long Taylor Swift album.

The book I'm reading at the moment is also a bookselling memoir. The author begins with the disclaimer: 'To protect the privacy of others, names and events have been changed, characters composited and incidents condensed.' Mostly I don't remember people's names. Nor all the incidents. As a result, I'm likely to expand on the ones I do recall, and take pride in using the real names of the people who feature wherever I can. Compositing characters sounds very clever, but slightly beyond my storytelling means. If you don't mind — and as I'm quite short on characters in the first place — I'll keep all identities separate.

This leaves us with just two main persons — a dumb bookseller and a dumb boat. I use the term 'dumb' differently in both instances. Where it describes the boat, it refers only to his lack of chat and not to meagre intelligence. I set great store by Joseph's brains. The bookseller's is another matter.

How I met Joseph is a very modern love story. We found each other online. On the Google search engine, to be precise. I had entered 'Narrow boat for sale' and there was a picture of Joseph, who lived in Warwick at the time, hanging out on the side of the Grand Union dressed all in black, which is a French existential look I particularly dig. After a flurry of emails we arranged to meet up. It was late January 2009 when I first saw him. As invariably happens, the profile photo he'd posted wasn't quite the whole picture. Joseph had cardboard blinkers over the bow windows and a measles of rust above the waterline. Threads of frost were laid out over the grill of a three-legged BBQ stand, which stood extraneously against the front door. But the black lip over his roof was warm to touch, and it was as though the numbed sun had stretched out its fingers to him as well because his sides were clutched with darts of pale light. I wanted to never let go. Joseph was £25,000 and that much money made me cold again, for I had no idea where to find it.

Who knows what Joseph's first impressions of me were. He never speaks of it. I can tell you how things appear at this stage of our tale though. I am twenty-seven years old and my hair is still clean (this is day one). However, my attire is already what can only be politely described as 'principal boy'. While girls in tights may have been salacious to pantomime audiences circa the early twentieth century, my new wardrobe of black leggings and mid-calf sailing boots, accompanied by the Croydon facelift of pulled-back tresses, is as far from sexy Peter Pan as Pol Pot from a peace prize. For 'dressed-up' days, I have a pair of elastic-waisted jeans. That's not to say I didn't pack a more feminine trousseau, too. It's just that the Aire and Calder Navigation et al don't afford much opportunity to wear hot pants and halter-neck bikinis unremarked.

My friend Graeme meets me one lunchtime near the end of the trip in Newark. It had been a late night and an early start so I'd left my leggings on for bed, but put silk pyjamas over. In the morning it briefly looked like rain, so blue waterproof trousers went over both of these, and knee-high socks and boots. Plastic Morrisons bags fastened by the handles were employed over the boots and socks because I was fed up of rain finding new ways to dampen my toes. On top I wore a grey T-shirt with yaks on, which said 'Yak, Yak, Yak, Yak, Yak Tibet'. This clearly marked something of a merchandising departure for Tibet when I bought it in Llasa five years earlier. Previously, my brother had spent time in the region, and his souvenir haul was definitely still of the 'Free Tibet' ilk. On top of this I had four hooded jumpers, a duffel coat and — unusually — a life jacket. For reasons I'll explain later, death had been very nigh just twelve hours before and I was now a new fan of the buoyancy aid. 'Sarah,' Graeme says, when he finds me unpeeling hoods from my greasy ponytail, 'I've seen you in many strange and unflattering clothes these past few months, and I've never said anything that would hurt you. But this . . . ' he waves his hands towards me sadly, 'This is a new low.'

I digress. We were on our way to Stratford-upon-Avon . . .

7

GREEN

What I am swiftly discovering on the way is that, while the book sufficiency model neatly bypasses monetary failings, it can't mask my incompetence at the helm of a narrow boat. I quickly realise that bribing passers-by with free books to work the locks for me will be unsustainably costly. There are over 700 of these hell chambers on my circuitous route around England and Wales. At the rate I'm going (a £7.99 paperback per paddle), I'll have to explain a £22,372 stock deficit to my accountant by the time six months are up. The fact that I haven't been able to afford an accountant since the shop opened is hardly a consolation. I will have to explain it to *someone*. And it will be acutely embarrassing.

A lock, for anyone not initiated in the ways of the inland waterways, can be described thus: the devil's work. They exist to carry water up — or downhill — and to make what would otherwise be a lovely day's boating positively penitential. I don't use these religious terms loosely. Working a lock single-handed is akin to corporal mortification. Like wearing a cilice or flagellation, it's a very painful and very public way of being punished for 'natural' sin. In this case, topography.

Awkward, heavy, slow and prone to dirty your clothes beyond the redemptive powers of Persil, locks are a truly male invention. And only men, you soon discover on the canals, have any fondness for the sport. There is good reason for this: apart from their strange brains being oddly fascinated by the mechanics of a lock (although anyone who's ever witnessed a bath fill up should be reasonably over the novelty by now), they rarely do the hard work themselves. Rather, it's the waterways WAGs doing the real sweat. You'll see these ill-used women tipped off their vessel at least a half-mile before the approaching lock. Having jumped the Beechers Brook of swamp and nettle bouquet between boat and towpath, they'll brush off their muddied palms, grimace at the sprained ankle and begin an inelegant trot towards the three-ton gate on the horizon.

At the start of my journey I had little idea how to respond to the obvious unfairness of this arrangement. Lock paddles are bastards to wind up and, unless you possess the glutes of Geoff Capes, shoving open the gates with your bum is equally trying. On face value, seeing pensionable women effectively caber-tossing their way through these unhallowed barriers should be a triumph for women's liberation. Here we are, no longer shaking our ass to degrading Renault Mégane ads, but putting our buttocks to men's work. Moving timber with our tush? We can do it! Hell, we can even *multitask* with a mobile phone to our ear and a dock leaf poultice soothing stung shins.

But there's something nevertheless unset-tling at the sight. Something Not Quite Right when you meet this politically correct pastoral scene for the umpteenth time chugging round a bend in rural Warwickshire with only grazing sheep to direct questions of gender bias to. Well, not *wholly* true. It's 2011. I have Caitlin Moran's *How to be a Woman* sitting hardbacked and kickass on a shelf, freshly published and polemical. Her rule of thumb is pretty damning: 'You can tell whether some misogynistic societal pressure is being exerted on women by calmly enquiring, 'And are the men doing this, as well?' If they aren't, chances are you're dealing with what we strident feminists refer to as 'some total fucking bullshit'.' South of Birmingham I share a lock with a couple whose captain actually apologises for his wife being so slow between paddles. She's hip-to-toe in plaster cast and, at that precise moment, wavering precariously over the half-full chamber on a gate crossing three times narrower than her encased limb. 'It comes off next week, thank God. Might actually make some progress then,' he mutters.

That most of these women insist they'd rather be doing the hard work than sitting astern glugging Chardonnay and nonchalantly twiddling the tiller in the right direction with their big toe is fallacy. They have been mistakenly told, as with cars, that squeezing vehicles into small spaces is 'difficult' and therefore something to avoid. 'Not easy', perhaps. But relatively? When the only other option requires steroid injections in your posterior to carry out with any poise? I know which I'd rather. And after practice, if not a piece of piss, you're at least adopting a seasoned 'ready position' when the jolt of steel pranging brickwork threatens to tip the wine bottle overboard.

I'm not *quite* at that stage yet. And I still haven't fully grasped how to stop the boat. On approaching a lock, I leap off clutching the rear rope, wrap it round the nearest mooring stump, and hold on for dear life while the boat comes to a twanging, shuddering halt and then drifts noseward to the other bank, blocking all traffic coming out of the lock. Having been politely told that tying up with the middle rope would at least keep the boat parallel to the correct side, I assume a little more professionalism in this manoeuvre, but still manage to smash the hatch window clean out of its frame when I get the rope caught around an open metal shutter, which slams closed. Later, reverse gear and bow thrusters are employed, and this cuts glazing bills and finger injuries considerably.

Having halted and tied up the boat (my knots are elaborate but largely ineffectual), I begin the trudge, metal windlass in hand, to the lock. Here begins the laborious process of emptying or filling it, returning to the boat, navigating into the lock, jumping back off to close the gate, winding up paddles to let water in or out, leaping back on the boat to keep it from slamming into gates with the force of rushing water, off again to open the gates, on to steer out, mooring the other side and running back to close the gates. The system gobbles time as pandas do bamboo — inefficiently, greedily, but gratefully, without the need to produce forty poos a day. The longest I ever spend working a lock is

120 minutes. People run half-marathons or watch feature films faster.

Throughout The Book Barge's voyages, locks are to me what dragon episodes seem to chivalric knights in Old English romances. They are trials. They are tests. If not of honour (I approach them with cowardice), at least of stubbornness (which I have in Taurean bucketfuls). There is one romance in particular I draw constant mental comparisons to — a late fourteenth-century alliterative poem with illusions of Arthurian grandeur, but written in my native North West Midlands dialect and with a deeply flawed hero. His name alone is reassuringly chav — an ugly hybrid of Gav and Wayne, which wouldn't look out of place on the credits of TOWIE. Gawain (*Sir* Gawain, to give him his correct title), is a knight of the Round Table. One Christmas, while feasting with his fellow horsemen, he rashly accepts a challenge from a mysteriously hued visitor to play a beheading game. As the name suggests, it's not exactly standard festive entertainment. No charades or Monopoly contests in Camelot, it seems. Instead, Gawain must strike the guest's unhealthily green head off and accept that he will suffer the same fate himself in exactly a year and a day.

What follows is effectively a beautiful

nature poem and a playful swipe at the high standards demanded by chivalric codes. Gawain has the usual battles with bulls and bears ('sometimes with savage boars, / And giants from the high fells'). He 'wars with dragons, or with wolves,' and with 'wodwos' too, whatever they are. But these encounters are only mentioned in passing. The poet is more concerned with the journey, the duller day-to-day experience. The way 'He turns down dreary ways / Where dark hillsides lean, / His mood changing as the day's, / But the chapel could not be seen.' If anyone doubts the relevance of Old English sagas to twenty-first-century existence, let him spend just half a day on the Coventry Canal to realise the brutal, unmitigated truth of that exquisite quatrain.

The chapel episode comes at the very end, and shows Gawain as scared, fallible and wholly *human* when he jerks his head away to avoid the axe blow he's had coming the whole adventure. John Milton wrote that this is one of the highest achievements of romance literature: 'Assuredly we bring not innocence into the world, we bring impurity much rather: that which purifies us is trial, and trial is by what is contrary.' The grime of experience, I hope, will do the same to me. My silted fingernails tell a different story.

Yet every time I approach a lock gate I think of the detail of Gawain's final showdown: the 'rushing waterfall', the 'deep dark of a cave', 'a desolation, / With its sinister shrine, and tufts of weed everywhere'. I wonder then at the unknown poet's prescience. It seems uncanny, writing hundreds of years before another local boy, James Brindley, had started buckling them to our rivers, that someone could sum the horror of these places so succinctly. 'What an unhappy place!' I sob, knotting my armoured steed to a rough branch. 'An evil chapel.' I stalk over to the mound and channel all Gawain's despair in the satanic plea: 'Devil / Take this accursed church, the worst I've ever chanced on.'

8

STRATFORD

Stratford should be the grail for floating bookshops. There's the Shakespeare connection, theatres, tourists, a canal basin bang in the centre and a public washroom. As it happens, the washroom is the only thing that delivers. I'm moored by the new glassy playhouse but all I can truly appreciate is the red brick toilet and shower block around the corner from McDonalds, where I stand in line behind a fifteen-year-old pinking her hair with a home dye kit. Her friend, less curiously coiffed, asks me if I'm homeless. At this point the first girl accidentally snorts some cochineal up her nose so the conversation dies because she's crying.

Note to other town planners: less money on Shard-like structures, more on the low-level showers. I visit them every day. I think it's because I'm so shiny-looking and happy on the boat now that a Japanese customer mistakes me for a descendant of Shakespeare. I just nod and smile while she takes some pictures because I don't like disappointing people. It's like when drivers pull over when you're trying to walk somewhere and ask for directions and you haven't got a clue but feel obliged to make something up anyway. 'Left at the traffic lights, first left, then immediate right. On the corner. By the big Tesco.' They seem so pleased with me.

One man who isn't is the British Waterways guy in charge of Bancroft Basin, where I'm moored. I'm tied up next to a gallery boat, and there's an ice-cream-vending vessel nearby too. Sandwiched between art and Fabs like this makes me feel that life is finally happening for me. My place seems obvious. Despite that, I'm woken early on my first morning by a rapping on the back hatch. I try to ignore it but the man's shouting 'I know you're in there and you shouldn't be,' so I crawl out the front guiltily and go over to see what he has to say. It's not great news. The spot's for permanent traders only — people who pay local authorities for a licence to be there — and I'll have to move to the pontoons on the other side where customers will be even scarcer and the Magnum freezer further. Because the thought of this makes me so sad inside, I lie and tell him I have special permission from the head of British Waterways to be there. As under cross-examination I'm not clear who the head of

British Waterways is, I capitulate and name the regional trading manager of the organisation instead, who I once met two years ago. Prosecution retires to his British Waterways van to ring for confirmation. I reluctantly start the engine. When he comes back though, it seems everything's okay, which freaks me out a bit. I can stay for a week.

Ian, the British Waterways man, is nice after that and comes over to chat every day or so. Alan, on the Barge Gallery, is equally generous and so if I'm not visiting Helen and Andy's boat on the river, I'm talking to Alan or Ian or one of the buskers. Even though I'm not selling or swapping much, the sun's out and people smile, and my picture's in the *Stratford Herald*, albeit two weeks after I've departed.

I like it best in the evening. I take walks along the river or say hi to Hamlet, who I haven't given much thought to since sixth form. He looks pissed off still. He's statued with his head in one hand, Yorick's in the other. I thought he might be interested to know what's happened in Denmark since he was slaughtered there and resurrected in bronze in Warwickshire. I tell him about Carlsberg and how it's probably the best beer in the world, and about his country's part in the Great Northern War with Peter the Great.

'Hey, Hamlet', I say, 'if Peter the Great brought out a range of FUDs, what do you suppose they'd be called?' Hamlet has no idea. 'PeeGees!' I squeal. Hamlet just puts his head in his hands.

The second time I visit Hamlet, I'm more sober. I've been thinking about the girl in the washrooms who asked if I was homeless. I have now admitted to myself that I am. I want to talk to Hamlet about our generation because he's a boomerang child too and had to move back in with his mum and step-dad when he finished uni. I'm full of data and new theories on why Hamlet's so moody all the time in his play. According to the Office for National Statistics, nearly three million British adults aged twenty to thirty-four live with their parents in 2011, up 20 per cent since 1997. Most of these struggle to readjust to domestic expectations after the liberties of student life or a rented house. I suggest it might make us a bit grumpy from time to time. I offer this as an explanation of why Hamlet has such a tense relationship with his parents. 'You're unemployed because your uncle succeeded your father to the throne,' I recount. 'No job equals no means to move out. You feel trapped. Your self-esteem has taken a blow. Hold my hand, Hamlet, we're in this together.' I reach out but he won't take it. 'Fine, be like that,' I storm. 'Do you know what the difference between you and me is, Hamlet? We're both spoilt, pampered adultescents too used to getting our own way. But at least I *know* I'm an adultescent and not some tragic hero.' I quietly congratulate myself on getting the word 'adultescent' in. Shakespeare's going to be kicking himself for not inventing that peach among his 1,000-odd other new ones.

The final time I visit Hamlet I take him a verse I wrote when there were no customers on the boat. I had a lot of time to spend over it. It's called Depression. I clear my throat: 'On really bad days I think all the world's a turd / And all the men and women merely arseholes.'

'That's not poetry,' Hamlet says, all catty and rude about it.

'Yeah, well it wasn't supposed to be anyway,' I tell him. 'It's *pooetry* and there's a difference. Jeez, life doesn't have to be so downright serious all the time.' And with that I turn my back on Hamlet and start the engine and go.

'Wrong play as well,' he shouts after me. What a whiner.

9

Ms

At Hatton, on the Grand Union, there's a flight of twenty-one locks with a drop of forty-five metres. I quickly tire — these are wider locks than I am used to — and moor halfway down, about a two-minute walk from the café, where I can use the toilet in the day, and five minutes from the pub on the hill, where I clean my teeth in the evenings. Walking back to the boat in the dark, I can feel the whip of bats curling in and out of the trees.

Aside from with Helen and Andy and a couple of other people, I've not had much success swapping books. At Hatton I try to simplify things. I have a whiteboard on which I've scrawled that I'm willing to trade for pretty much anything, but now I narrow it down to just three demands. I call these the three 'Ms': milk, meals and aMusement. The last one needs a bit of work. I take a photo and post it on Twitter and Facebook, then hang the board above my desk and wait to see what happens.

The first breakthrough is a text from a guy who used to visit the boat back in Staffordshire. He did a GP training placement at the surgery near the marina and sometimes popped in at lunchtime. He read a lot of Alexandre Dumas. We used to talk about fencing and I showed him the fencing mask I kept over a lamp, which diced the light into hundreds of squares and threw them over the ceiling. When he finished his placement he used to write to me on the boat. Proper letters, handwritten; sentences that still held the scabs of crossings out and that pulled lazily to the right. On mornings like these, when the postman had thrown the letter down the stairs and I had a mug of tea to read it with, it felt a good life being a bookseller. There would be the latest delivery of books in a box by my feet, and afterwards I would take them all out slowly and separate the ones that customers had ordered and the ones that I had. That second pile, stacked clumsily with my eyes already back in the box for the next one, would arch all its spines to flaunt a body of creamy pages under the sharp tailoring of dust jackets and tight paper bindings.

I meet the guy later that day. He's in Warwick visiting a university friend and invites me out with them for food. The next day is equally fruitful. The towpath is busy with walkers and tourists and among the steady flow of customers is a woman called Annabel who offers food, shower and a bed. She looks like my sister. Her father, who's with her, makes me laugh at his excitement over my trip.

At Annabel's house I take a bath while she's cooking. She's left slippers out for me and a face mask. Lying in the bath, I can hear the pans and chopping downstairs and, from the open window, the closing of the day — the birds, the washing unpegged, the quickening pulse of a basketball left to bounce all alone. These are the sounds of home, of growing up at home. I put my head under and rattle the plug chain to remember the sound of our garage door closing.

When I'm finished I go downstairs to ask Annabel about the photographs on the bathroom wall, which look like a place in Ghana I visited once. She was there too, just a few months before me. We talk about the coincidence and I think of the book I was reading when I was there, which was *Anna Karenina*. It was being read to me, would be more accurate. I was on a long bus journey with a boy called John who I met on the newspaper we were both volunteering at, and he was reading aloud. As the sun started sliding down the window he stopped and looked at it with me. It's like the little ball that skips along karaoke lyrics, he said, and I wished I'd thought of that myself. Later, the bus stopped for a couple of hours so the driver could rest and eat. John lent me the book and I lay outside with one of those big bus wheels as a headboard and the book as a pillow and closed my eyes.

I loved *Anna Karenina* then and still do. I read all Tolstoy's other books, then Dostoevsky and Gogol and Chekhov, Pushkin and a Penguin book of Soviet short stories. And then at university I chose modules in Russian literature so I could read even more and write about them too. After that I got into Vladimir Sorokin and cried over Viktor Pelevin's Omon Ra, when he's pedalling a radio beacon across a false moon with 'special hydrocompensatory tampons' shoved up his nose. I watched my first opera because it was based on Mikhail Bulgakov's *The Heart of a Dog*. When I finally got round to rereading *Anna Karenina* after staying at Annabel's, I still loved it and still found new things to think about. Where are her parents? How was her childhood? Tolstoy skips this. She's fully formed and everyone else too. This bit appealed to me now because this is how I met Annabel, and she me. It was the same with all the other people I met over those six months. There was no context, no past, no younger self, no memories to cast long, late-afternoon shadows through the window.

Except in one case. On my penultimate day at Hatton Locks, British Waterways receive a complaint that I'm still moored in the pound between two locks, which isn't allowed. They send a young man out with strawberry-blond hair and sun-pinked cheeks to tell me to move on. When he knocks on the hatch I know him from somewhere. 'Murray, from school,' he helps, and we giggle at each other and call up all the people from our shared past. And it's all okay, except I have no milk to make him tea.

10

MARATHON (part i)

After Hatton I retrace my snail trail to Birmingham to take part in a canal boating marathon. It's an annual event organised by the Birmingham Canal Navigations Society but some years, when there isn't enough water in the system, they have to cancel — like the year before. As such, this year is a bigger event than normal. Twenty-two boats have entered. I want mine to win.

This, Andy Tidy has already explained, is easier said than done. Sitting on Wand'ring Bark on the Avon in Stratford I first float the idea of a canal boat competition. 'I think I'm getting quite *good* at this narrow boating lark,' I say with unusual modesty. 'I just want some way of proving it. Fancy a race?' Andy gives the suggestion some thought, which throws me a bit. 'Well, we *could* . . . How are you fixed for the end of the month?' I put all onward travel plans on hold, become a paid-up member of the organising society and listen gleefully while he refills my glass with home brew and tells me the story of the marathon.

Because Birmingham has little else to recommend it, us Midlanders often like to tell visitors that the city has more canals than Venice. We say it proudly. It conjures pleasant images of gondolas and romance and isn't entirely untrue. At their height, the Birmingham Canal Navigations extended for approximately 160 miles. They were limbed with private branches too, arms and basins serving the multitude of new industry that had sprung up in the area. Over the last century, this has reduced to just 100 miles, of which much is underused and virtually unnavigable. The marathon was introduced as a way of increasing traffic on the network, a 'use it or lose it' last-ditch effort to keep a little of the city's watery history alive. There are also other benefits. By requesting that participants record any difficulties they encounter during the competition, the BCNS can isolate parts of the system that need particular or urgent attention. They submit a report to British Waterways after the event, requesting that these problems be addressed.

The marathon is a particularly complicated race to score. A master spreadsheet tallying all the competitors' variables takes at least two weeks to decipher before a winner can be announced. Points are allocated depending on route difficulty, crew size, length and draught of boat, starting point, locks encountered and for reaching the finishing line in Walsall before 2 p.m. To make the thirty-hour trudge more 'fun', there's also a treasure hunt element to accrue bonus points.

On paper, it looks like I should maximise the bonus opportunities and compete single-handed. I can score one extra point per two locks, plus another for every five miles completed. According to the nine-page rule book, this exists to 'reflect the increased difficulty when mooring for locks, looking for clues, having a warm drink, etc.' However great the temptation though, there's also the high probability I'll run aground on a submerged Ford Cortina. For this I'll need brawn.

I tentatively ask Stu if he's free that weekend. The truth is, I miss him. We still text each other, talk, but the more hours I spend at the tiller, the more I feel the miles that have opened between us. On the phone, all the small things I store up each day to tell him seem to spill out between strained silence, so that it becomes easier to simply withhold them. I tell him I filled up with diesel for the first time; that I shared a ham sandwich and a can of pop with some walkers at lunch. But not about my quiet pride at being able to manoeuvre backwards into the space at the pump. Not about how, when one of the walkers apologised for the thick butter on the roll, it made me suddenly sad to remember all the times Stu had grimaced at my own awkward way of spreading bread. When I ask him to help with the marathon, I don't expect him to say yes.

Aside from the page detailing infection risks, I don't spend too much time reading the rest of the information book beforehand. The leptospirosis details I find macabrely exciting. Do not put wet ropes, fishing lines or other objects in your mouth, I mentally note. Do not handle hypodermic needles. In the event of an outbreak of avian flu, seek medical advice if you inadvertently handle a bird carcass. I'm all prepped and positioned centrally near Gas Street Basin when 8 a.m. comes on Saturday, 28 May and we can finally open the sealed envelope with the cruise log and question sheet. I start the engine.

This is when I become aware that book-shop customers are like buses. It's an overused simile but it's 8 a.m. You wait three years, they come three at once. They take bloody ages and they don't read books. Another one comes down the steps and I'm trying to hurry them all up but they've started asking why my plants are dead and for permission to take pictures of each other pretending to read. Stu walks off somewhere. Some more people come.

One of them picks up a Book Barge at Large flyer, detailing my desire to swap stock for staple foods and offers me free mojitos at Brindley Place. He doesn't want any books in return because he doesn't read. I give up. I get on the Cuban rum bus all the way to 8 p.m.

Although we're now twelve hours behind the other competitors, I have a new game plan and great confidence in it. We'll head straight to Walsall by the most direct route but make it in a *record-breaking time*. This will wow the committee, I am certain. They will garland our bow with mint and lime wedges and sugar our entry with triple-letter scores. Stu tells me this doesn't make sense and could I shut up while he listens to the Champion's League final, which the wind is blowing away. While Stu takes the tiller, I root his radio among the dead plants to firm it against the gust and this works well. But even so, when there are goals, the wind blowing and the engine blowing too make the noise from the radio small. The whole stadium is contained.

When Barcelona win we carry on. We make black waves for my camera to film. When it drizzles I text Andy and we detour to intercept his boat. He throws across a big golfing umbrella, navy and white. We take turns to hold it up and bib the sky until nothing more dribbles down except the dark.

At 10 p.m. we moor in a flight of locks by an arm of canal that is closed because of chemical pollution. It colours the black water all the shades of dead rainbows when we cut through it. Tying up the boat I can see the pink Care Bear of my sister's childhood in it, whose tummy symbol was a rainbow. I look for the double rainbow I saw once over the Wear in Durham and all the other rainbows I've ever spotted from car windows. They're all in there, slicked by the black but colouring through. There are reefs of them, I suspect, more beautiful than the seas in there. They unspool their red-purples and green-greys and yellow-golds and brown-violets all over the underwater until the display makes me drowsy.

Before we sleep, two men talk to us. They're walking to the pub. They tell us that just a few months ago a boat was torched here. It's a bad spot, they say. We should move on. But we can't be bothered and we get into sleeping bags. When my eyes close Stu's stay open a long time, his green-greys in the black, his hand around the metal tiller pin we've brought inside. He listens to the murmurs of all the people who walk past.

We don't burn in our boat. At some point

in the night though another goes past us. Stu is already up and by the window. When he moves the black curtain aside it lets the beam of the crew's head torches in and we're ashamed we haven't put their effort into our race too. But we'll make it in record-breaking time, I remind Stu. But this method still doesn't make sense and we sleep confused.

In the morning, going fast, Stu reads me sections 1.4 and sections 1.5 of the rule book. They state: *All British waterways by-laws, rules and regulations governing the use of boats on canals must be adhered to at all times, including the correct use of locks and observance of speed limits.* I slow the boat a little. He continues: *The average speed of powered craft can be calculated. Entrants whose average speed is in excess of British Waterways limits may have their points total reduced or be disqualified.*

So we drift imperceptibly towards Walsall, helped by all the arms of weed that band our propeller. We put our own hands in long rubber gloves to feel them away when they're too many. I start to like this canal and the ruined faces of the buildings we pass. Their windows are brown mirrors. They take our reflection and hold it — a boy and a girl and a long boat with a fuzzy green roof. Then they pass it on to their neighbour. We're whispered along like this until the last window, which is missing a pane, and then the sense of us is lost to them. When I look back they have fallen apart. They pick up the pieces and try them in different places but they can't remember how they once looked in the mirror of the dead water and we can't either.

We rack up six hours of cruising in total. We have slept or drunk the mojitos for twenty-four. Nevertheless, we receive a brass plaque — every participant does — and this goes in my handbag before we breakfast and then turn back to Birmingham in the rain.

The marathon is eventually won by a man called John Hammond on his narrow boat, Muskrat. In American-Indian creation myths, it is the muskrat that dives to the bottom of the primordial sea to bring up the mud from which the Earth is created. All the other animals failed.

11

MARATHON (part ii)

In the Summer 2011 issue of Boundary Post, the journal of the Birmingham Canal Navigations (BCN) Society, the Chairman's Report notes: John also won the award in 2009 so I think we shall have to design an exploding shopping trolley to slow him down a bit next year.

12

MARATHON (part iii)

In the same Summer 2011 issue of Boundary Post, the journal of the Birmingham Canal Navigations (BCN) Society, the report continues: The challenge was carried out in a spirit of cheerfulness and helpfulness. No one had to be towed in. Nineteen boats out of the twenty-two finished in Walsall Town Arm, where they were greeted by the Mayor and Mayoress of Walsall, Councillor Garry Perry and Mrs June Perry.

I'm reading this aloud to Stu a month after the event has happened. 'Does anything in that last sentence strike you as odd?' I ask, perplexed. 'Yes,' he nods thoughtfully. 'Nineteen boats out of the twenty-two finished. Yet we finished . . . in *twentieth* place. So we were beaten by a non-finisher?'

13

BICYCLE (part i)

I take the boat to a place called Kingswood Junction where my friend Narsh has promised to carry it on for me to Leamington Spa. He suspects he'll do a better job at selling books than I, and he does. Meanwhile, I catch a train to Cardigan Bay in Wales with a brutish-looking 1930s delivery bike to meet a man named Rob Penn for a different sort of mobile bookselling.

For thousands of years people who lived outside of cities or university towns relied on the travelling bookseller for their reading material. Dressed garishly to attract more attention, these strange figures trudged from village to village on foot, hauling their wares in baskets slung over their bellies or, in the case of the infinitely more dedicated Chinese, six-foot wooden shelving units strapped to their backs and decked with flags and ribbons. This nomadic retail has fascinated me for years. It has something of the missionary zeal to it. Having grown up wanting to be a saint, this is enough to recommend itself to me.

The saint thing, like most of my fancies, began with a book. I was raised Catholic, attended a convent school run by an order of strict German nuns and, on receiving my First Holy Communion aged seven, was gifted a glow-in-the-dark rosary — and a children's book of popular saints. These tales of ordinary people put on godly pedestals enthralled me. I suppose, like the reality shows kids grow up with today, they made the road to celebrity suddenly look relatively easy. It seemed a more achievable career than, say, becoming an aviatrix or solving a murder with a tin-can telephone and invisible ink pen, which were two other contemporary aspirations. As far as I could make out, I could become a female saint simply by following another trio of 'Ms': refusing Marriage, avoiding Money and Moving around the country obnoxiously pointing out the error of people's ways. With my virginity then still intact and just a jam jar of coppers to my name, I was confident Pope John Paul would beatify me just as soon as I set out with my road map. There was of course a fourth qualification I was more reluctant to investigate, which was to take full advantage of the first Martyrdom opportunity that presented itself.

You would think that twenty years and a noticeably reduced religious fervour would put paid to this fantasy of wandering the land, gospel in hand. However, my month of bookshop transit seems merely to have inflamed the idea. When I read in a Penguin newsletter that one of their authors is organising a bike ride to Hay-on-Wye to promote his new book, I'm overwhelmed by a strong desire to get in touch begging to squire. I will simultaneously mule and flog his books along the way, the letter of introduction reads. We'll save all heathen souls we meet en route for the reasonable cover price of just £7.99. He generously accepts. The book in question has a satisfyingly dogmatic title: *It's All About the Bike*. Rob's prologue rousingly preaches: 'If you have ever, just once, sat on a bicycle with a singing heart and felt *like an ordinary human touching the gods* [my italics], then we share something fundamental.'

As with most things, the devil is in the detail. How to pedal from beach to border in just four days and furnished with a small bookshop preoccupies me for hours. I briefly consider imitating the Olde Asian way and strapping one of Ikea's ubiquitous Billy bookcases from my shoulders. Or I could fashion some sort of side cart around my

Raleigh ladies' shopper. Just in time, I remember another ill-considered eBay purchase and rush to my parents' garage to dust down the black tradesman's bike I bought two years previously. It has rod brakes and a tiny front wheel that timorously moons the planetary one behind it. There are no gears and I seem to remember Rob mentioning something about the Cambrian mountains obstructing our route. If this is the case, gears would almost certainly be useful, I acknowledge, as would a considerably lighter frame.

But the positives surely outweigh these minor concerns. The bike has an enormous front basket to shelve the box of paperbacks I've just ordered, and its saddle is generously wide and springy. It's also been Book Barge branded so the advertising potential alone when it's finally parked outside the Hay Festival will be worth any muscle strain over the odd mountain or three. I start reading H G Wells's joyful *The Wheels of Chance* and anticipate the upcoming two-wheeled holiday as a similarly pleasant story of mild adventure and largely flat terrain. Wells, once described as the writer laureate of cyclists, states in that book that 'self-deception is the anaesthetic of life, while God is carving out our beings'.

Interlude for 'The Lives of the Saints:
Sarah of Book Barge'

Sarah of Book Barge (born Sarah Louise
Henshaw, 10th May 1983) was an English
book botherer and lay(about)woman.

When she was twenty-seven she gave up
(lost through business mismanagement) all of
her worldly possessions and credit rating and
lived instead by The Book. She travelled from
town to town, preaching against the evils of
Kindle and receiving many Victoria sponge
cakes.

Once, while she was sleeping on the
Regents Canal in Islington, she had a vision
that a drunk had untied her mooring ropes.
When she looked out of the porthole, she
discovered that a drunk had indeed untied
her mooring ropes.

To date, she has never cried tears of blood.
But she did once snort vodka off a teaspoon
and this made her eyes run voluminously as
The Spirit moved within her.

She was officially canalised on 20th
September 2011, when she fell into the
Castlefield Basin in Manchester after a night
out. Miraculously, she managed to grab hold
of the boat's gunwales on the way down, and
as such escaped a full immersion baptism.
This brush with Weil's Disease prompted her

to set up a colony for other rat wee paranoids, which she called *The Burton Literary and Rodent Pee Die Society*, which sounds like an excellent title for a bestseller. Having pitched it, she is reported to have exclaimed: 'Knock and the agent's door shall be slammed in your face.' She is venerated by other unsuccessful/wannabe novelists as a mystic for this bleak interpretation of the publishing industry.

She is survived by the Kobo.

14

BICYCLE (part ii)

Something that does worry me is my fitness. While I used to bike regularly to the boat when it was moored in the marina, I swapped for the wheels of the number 7 bus when I moved back in with my parents, who live further away. What little stamina I once built has sinkholed, and my face falls, too, just thinking about the 120-mile pedal. When I see the other riders with their exotic Lycra skins and the beautiful curved horns of their handlebars, I feel — as Hemingway must have felt on that first African safari — a violent blood lust to shoot and taxidermy the lot of them, these terrible, dangerous creatures.

Instead I grit my teeth and channel the Pollyanna of saints, Julian of Norwich. Julian was a similar age to me when she also looked death in the eye. She was severely ill and had almost given up on life when she had a series of intense visions in which God apparently told her that: 'All shall be well, and all shall be well, and all manner of thing shall be well.'

It's not the pithiest of catchphrases but has a certain Bruce Forsythian je ne sais quoi to it that I like. Julian seemed to like it too. She wrote it down, alongside other spiritual dialogues, in what is believed to be the first book written in the English language by a woman.

Julian had lots of other interesting things to say, including that in order to learn we must first fail. In order to fail, we inevitably have to sin. Although thousands of writers have added to the female literary canon since she became its mother, I can't help but think her twin themes of a) everything working out fine and b) not being too hard on yourself in the meantime are still the most important things I've ever read.

All *is* well, in the end. I know it as soon as we start and the sun drums a march on my skin. There's ice cream at Conti's in Lampeter, swimming in the Elan Valley. Between, the pedals make puppets of our legs and I smile to watch it from the back of the peloton. When it comes to hills, sometimes one of the men will take my bike ahead for me, and I ride theirs. Sometimes I just push it up, my arms out and head down as if I'm about to dive into the grey wave of the road.

It's a happy time. I sell a few books right away and buy a pair of white-rimmed plastic sunglasses and a German typewriter that I make up a story about having wanted for ages. In fact, I just feel stupid about the purchase because it's heavy and my legs hurt enough without the extra weight in the basket. In one town we stop for lunch at a pub and sit on the picnic tables out front. A group of seventeen- or eighteen-year-olds are drinking at the one next to us and giving us bad looks. Maybe it's because all our bikes are knotted in a messy pile or because we look so sweaty or something. I ask them if they want to buy a book and they laugh and joke about it uneasily but club together and buy one anyway. When Rob comes back from the bar they call him over to their table to write in his book. He has to write all their names, which are Welsh and difficult to spell. They bunch round and tell him each letter and he repeats them first before putting them down. We laugh on our table because he's sweating more than when he's on his bike.

On the last day we stop mid-morning for a snack. Rob's son and another boy come up with a game. They roll a hard-boiled egg from the grass verge into the centre of the road and wait for a car to squash it. It makes us all giggle to begin with, but the cars keep missing it and we get more and more tense watching. When a car tyre gets close, the egg sometimes rolls back a little from the breeze that's created. When this happens I think the egg looks like a great matador. Eventually a truck comes along and we boo because the egg doesn't stand a chance. When we get back on our bikes Rob cycles on ahead for his talk at the festival.

I arrive there too exhausted to stand easily but get inside the tent just before Rob starts. When he comes on I only hear the beginning of the talk — him reading from his book about why he rides a bike and hearing his boy laugh — and then I'm asleep and dreaming of a French writer called Alfred Jarry, and how everyone laughed at him when he painted his face green and rode through town on a bicycle. I join him on mine but I'm red, not green, from the clumsy brushstrokes of the sun and my lips coasted by red wine. I half awake to remember a story he wrote — *The Passion Considered as an Uphill Bicycle Race* — with Jesus's ordinary single-tube racing tyre punctured by a bed of thorns on the Golgotha course of fourteen turns. 'It is not true that there were any nails,' Jarry wrote. And now Rob's talking again and he's talking about my bike, 'that beast', how it came from Cardigan with us, and that I must stand up please, I must stand up and take applause for that bike. And I do. People clap and grin and my mouth pulls up too in the sleepy smile of a saint.

Before leaving Hay-on-Wye I buy a big old perambulator from an antique shop on the way out of town. I think that if I ever lose my boat or my bike I can carry some books easily enough in this and push them from town to town. I'm not thinking right. I get the boat keys back off Narsh at Leamington Spa, and move the shop along the canal to a little village in Warwickshire called Radford Semele because a British Waterways man has told me it'll be safer. By this time one of my arms is twice the size of normal and angry red at the sun that's been wheeling over me in Wales. I decide to take a short break, catch a lift home, and sleep for two days before my mum drives me back to the boat with my pram and proportional limbs again.

15

'SWOUNDS!

For several weeks I had a beautiful bonded-leather binding edition of *The Count of Monte Cristo* in the shop. This was some time before I moved the boat so I got it in for me really, as at the time I couldn't imagine anyone coming to Barton Marina and spending £25 actually buying one of my books. It had a satin ribbon bookmark and gilt edging to the pages. There were 1,072 pages and they all had that gold framing. I liked how it looked on the shelf in the boat, taller and wider than the other books alphabetised under D. Your eye was instantly drawn to it and lots of people picked it up and remarked how beautiful it was.

One day a woman came in with her daughter. Her daughter, who was sixteen, had visited before and we had talked about our favourite books. She reminded me of this when she came up to my desk clutching *The Count of Monte Cristo*. 'This is the book you told me I should read,' she smiled. 'I'd like to buy it.' I was inexplicably upset that, out of all the titles I had mentioned that day, she had to remember the Dumas one and had to pick up *that* edition. I really loved that book. 'It's an awful lot of money,' I said. 'Why don't you take the paperback one next to it. Or I could source you a really cheap secondhand version for just £2 or £3.'

'It's OK,' she laughed, 'I don't mind paying for this one. Look how pretty it is, Mum,' and she drew her mother towards the desk too.

We were now all three of us looking at this book with the handsome blue spine and the shimmering pages. When the girl traced her fingers over the front I couldn't help myself and snatched it away from under the fumbling whorls of her skin. 'Why don't you think about it first for a few days?' I found myself saying calmly. 'It'll still be here if you come back. I won't let anyone else have it.' Puzzled, the two women left.

Her mother returned a week later and silently picked it off the shelf again. When she brought it to the desk I pleaded with my eyes but she was firm and paid in cash, quickly. I felt like she had stolen something from me, but this was stupid because it's a shop and books are supposed to leave, like this.

I'm telling you this story because when I'm walking to the boat with my own mum and my new old pram and my arm that's shrunk back to size after the sunburn, I see immediately that something *has* been stolen. The lock on the back hatch is cut and one of the curtains inside has been pulled down. When I slide open the hatch and look down the stairs I see how everything has been touched and all the mess they made doing it.

The first thing I want to do is start the engine and move far away from Radford Semele. I want to keep moving, to see the wagging tail of water behind my boat and everything straight and solemn ahead of us. Although we don't go fast and we're never more than a leap from the towpath, still nothing like this touches us when we're moving.

But my mum makes me call the police and while I'm doing that she heads over to the only other boat we can see, which is moored about twenty-five metres in front of us. When I get off the phone I try the engine but they've been in there, too, and wires are chopped and things are missing, although I can't tell what because I never knew anything about the engine more than its colour. It is blue. My mum comes back quickly and scared-looking. 'There are at least two men on there', she tells me, 'and they threatened to set their dogs on me. I just wanted to know if they heard anything,' she said.

We sit on the bow of the boat and wait for the police. After a couple of minutes the two men from the other boat come over, without their dogs. I tell them that my boat's been burgled and they say they've also had things stolen — some fishing gear left outside, a couple of other things. But when I tell them they can report this to the police they remember their stuff was stolen last month, and not in the last few days actually, and they won't need to bother the police.

I look straight at the taller man then and know. 'Why are you moored here?' I ask.

'Our engine is broken, we're waiting for a part.'

'Have you got it now?'

'Yes. Maybe. We need to fit it though.'

I carry on staring and my mum is doing it too now. The man says, 'So is this some sort of shop?'

'It's a bookshop.'

'Can I look round?'

'Not until the police have been.'

'It's a shame, I really wanted to buy the little book you have in the kids' section for my baby girl. The one with the horse on the cover. My baby girl would just love that.'

'But how do you know about that book?' I ask. 'You've never been inside.'

'Oh, you know, saw it from the window.'

But he can't because all the curtains are still up except for the one ripped down, at the other end of the boat.

I can hear my blood smashing, smashing, smashing inside. My hands are white because all that blood is rushing in to brawl too.

'I like your pram,' the shorter man says.

'Buy it.' They're surprised at this, but they don't argue.

'How much?'

I look at the pram, which still has the £15 price tag and now licks of mud from the towpath all over its sides and the torn hood. It's a horrible pram and the nonsense of buying it recalls my silliness over the Dumas book too. Vengeance is a difficult thing to put a price on. They pay me from the wad of cash Narsh made for me while I was in Wales. It was the second highest weekend takings since the shop opened. The tall man folds the rest back in his jeans pocket. The shorter one tries to shake my hand. 'No hard feelings, eh?' he says. They walk away in the direction of the road and we hear an engine start and then see a van pull over the hump of the bridge. We tell the police all this but my blood still kicks because nothing was done.

With no working engine, my mum helps me pull the boat out of Radford Semele with ropes. The dogs on the other boat take up their barking when we haul ours past. When she leaves I pick the emptied cash register from the floor and put it back on the desk. It's an old-fashioned one that makes a ring when you open the drawer. I open and shut it, open and shut it, again and again. It makes the sound of success. It's a lousy score for this scene. I put in the £25 I got for the old pram and shut it up.

16

OATS

In all they've taken £300 of cash, the black box that makes the heating system work, the black box that converts electrical current, damaged the engine and nicked a camera too. Book after book has been pushed along the plank of its shelf and tipped, flapping, to the floor below. They lie open and over each other, spines lined with their little traumas.

I get the boat to Long Itchington and spend a few days fixing things up. Stu makes me an oak bat to fend off other intruders but while I'm waiting for an engineer to arrive I swing at cereal bars with it instead. I have cupboards and cupboards of cereal bars that people seem to like gifting me. But I do not like cereal bars. I do not like cereal bars at all.

The engineer turns out to be hot and after he's gone I bat a few more Nutri-Grain bars across the canal, thinking about whether I should be sowing my oats in different ways. I take my laptop up to the pub to charge the battery and Google 'spreading your wild oats' to see what the internet has to say on the matter. A Mumsnet thread comes up discussing whether it's important to sleep around before settling down with one guy and is full of people dissing their friends' relationships, extolling their own and generally ignoring the question. That site is pretty confusing. They abbreviate everything. One of the problems I have with the oat thread is that it takes me a while to realise that DP stands for Darling/Dear Partner and not Displaced Person. It's a relief figuring it out. I was wondering how forced migration fitted into SWOI (shagging without intent — more Mumsnet lingo) and my mind was coming up with all sorts of bewildering images. I think I could have worked it out sooner if the darling/ dear sentiments had been more obvious to spot amid the vitriol. I look it up on the Mumsnet glossary for confirmation. Even with my extensive knowledge of toilet acronyms I still get freaked out by some of the letter combos they bandy around. Who knew egg-white cervical mucus (EWCM) could be brusqued, for example?

When my friends Laura and Graeme come out to visit me one night a week later we discuss it some more. I'm moored in Lower Heyford, a little Oxfordshire village of thatched homes walled caramel brown. It's tractable, neat — even the tall reeds that picket fence the bank by my boat. We all three sit on the lip of the bow behind them and watch the ducks' anxious swimming. Graeme thinks I should call the engineer back. He calls him Brian, for some reason, even though his name's different. After a while and a few drinks I can't remember his name either and call him Brian too. Graeme suggests Brian and I could get married and make canal babies. He thinks my romantic future lies with a dirty dredger man and not with a businessman or a gardener. I point out sniffily that Brian is quite clean actually, and not a dredger man but an engineer, but Graeme can't appreciate the distinction after half a bottle of Southern Comfort and gets bored and cycles back to his hotel.

Laura pours more drinks and the topic returns to relationships. More than anyone at the time, I think she understands why things finished with Stu and what I'm doing canalling about the country pretending to be in love with an engineer. We are a similar age and share the same enchantment with possibility. She's what I call a Committed Fickle too. Someone who sees the world for the buffet of choice it is, picking up a different finger food every five minutes and exclaiming over every cocktail sausage or blini: 'This will sate my appetite . . . No this

80

will. Or maybe just a mini pizza will do it.' And so we move from laden table to laden table, giggling wedding guests again, as we were when we first became friends. We sat opposite each other then, fiddling with the wine and chair cover corners and the place holders and anything else to take our mind from the tedium of speeches and thwart our guilty hiccups. And when we both looked up and recognised it, we couldn't stop the laughing, which spilt down our chins and piled in the skirt of our dresses.

That night in Lower Heyford we talk about our favourite subject, which is the future. She's become a climber and wants to give up her job to move to Wales. 'Let me come too,' I excitedly interject. We arrange how it will be there together and it's like Dylan Thomas described in *Fern Hill* — all running and hay bales and water and green. Frightened then that the evening is running out, I suggest setting light to the ornamental wooden boats I have on the shelves inside. We set them on the flat water, captained by a single match. We poke them with sticks to encourage them on their voyage. Out in the middle their fabric sails tack suddenly yellow in the dark. We cheer and whip the water with our branches. One by one the boats tip and the skim of the canal pats out their light.

Happy and sick we go to bed. The boat swings back and forth and at the crest of every upwards arc I fancy I can see the fields and the greener grass. Higher, higher; I want to jump into them. I squeal to Laura, who swings next to me. Our widening smiles describe the trajectory of our seats. And so the dream goes on until the present is exhausted and stops pushing us.

17

MILK

The next day ends more solemnly. Having said goodbye to Laura in the early afternoon I carry on down the Oxford Canal through the woods. There are fallen branches in the water and the shadows cast by the trees look like so many rats crawling over them. The sun is here and there and I'm doing my usual hopping from one bare foot to the other because the black steel floor gets so hot over the engine. It's a quiet section of the canal so my iPod goes in and I'm singing wildly and trying to turn my hopping into a dance. I sing a lot from the back of the boat. In tunnels I'll always belt tunes out and it drives away my great fear that the walls are getting closer and closer and that soon I'll be unable to stand upright and then the boat will be wedged in their grey dripping arms and the bodies of so many murder victims will rise up and choke me with their slimy hands. This is the power of music, to stamp terrors like this back down into the corpse-muddled canal bed.

Instead I think about all the lifeless people

in proper jobs while I'm lucked out singing Kate Bush songs on the back of a floating bookshop. And I think about what I *used* to imagine my dream job to be, which was a journalist, and how that turned out, which was badly. A job, I have discovered by this time, is a dull and dirty word. In professional wrestling the term 'job' describes a losing performance. We use 'job' to allude to criminal activity — a bank job — or, as children, to turds that won't flush. In the Bible it's the name of the unluckiest man. More unlucky even than Jonah, who was swallowed by a whale. In the Book of Job all of his possessions are destroyed. That includes 500 oxen and 500 donkeys (stolen), 7,000 sheep (burned) and 3,000 camels (another case of theft). Then a house collapse wipes out all his children. As Job comes to grips with this, Satan gets permission to make things a little more awful still by smiting Job with boils. There's a particularly horrendous scene where he's sat in a heap of ashes scraping his skin with broken pottery. Even on my worst day on the boat, which was when I overturned a watering can of my own urine and ate cold macaroni cheese and sold only two books, I still feel better than that.

So I keep singing under Cleeves Bridge and High Bush Bridge, even hauling the big gates open at Dashwood Lock. At North-brook Bridge I try steering into the corner without hands, the tiller nuzzled in the small of my back. I clap myself for completing it so well. Waiting for Northbrook Lock to empty, I stretch out on the black and white beam and feel the cashmere touch of sun on my bare legs and arms and grin at the faceless sky. I salute New Brighton Bridge and Old Brighton Bridge and the pipe bridge too by the disused quarry, and at Pigeon Lock near Kirtlington I tie up with my feet still tripping over these friendly names.

The birthday weather continues into the evening and I walk out to find some milk at the smallholding I passed by boat earlier. A track hedged with cricket pop leads there and I stop to listen because I haven't heard their comb wings strummed like this for a long time. As outdoor gigs go, it's right up there, even though crickets only have four hits. Two of them are about getting laid, one about having just been laid and the last is a really angry Rage Against the Machine-type one, which is meant to scare other guys off. From what I know about heavy metal it's usually the guys that buy into it so maybe they need to rethink their audience slightly. The tune I'm listening to sounds like one of the getting laid ones. There are Barry White influences in there for sure. I sit by the hedge for ten minutes or so and applaud politely before I get up. I can't say for sure if they hear. Crickets are weird like that. They have something called tympanic membranes in their knees to pick out other cricket song but I don't know how well these register with their human fan base.

When I get to the smallholding it's as beautiful as it looked from the canal. As well as chickens and a Jersey cow, there are a couple of Morris Minors, a cute caravan and some big wooden cart wheels pushed against the wall. Also some sort of outdoor kitchen and, around it, covered tables with fabric bunting and jam-jar lanterns looped in the trees over them. I can't help staring at everything and eventually a woman called Jane comes out to see what I'm doing. I tell her about the boat and needing milk and she claps her hands together as I've been doing all day and heaps cake on me too, plus a pair of scissors to cut sweet peas in her flower garden.

Jane also has a boat. She used to live on it with her wheelwright husband until they bought this land and slowly developed the outbuildings into more spacious accommodation. Now it serves as a very small shop for jams and preserves on Sunday afternoons, which is when Jane opens the farm for cream teas and lunches.

Walking back to the boat I can only think of one time when I was happier. When I turned twenty-one, Stu drove up to see me at uni. He had a tent in the car and we set it up in the dark on the riverbank and ate birthday cake with our legs plaited over the threshold zips. In the morning we walked back along the water like this, hands too full of gifts to hold each others'. Stu swung a CD player and I was teasing him for the song choice. He started bleating the words over the top with the sun sitting there on his shoulder, rolling eyes with me. We walked back to halls like this. Him singing to the morning, me barbed with my happiness. The sun just carried on sitting there all day.

I arrange the sweet peas in a vase on the floor by my sleeping bag and then sit out front with my milk while the night slides in. I don't think about the future or the past. Cross-legged on the metal floor, I fling my arm over the side of Joseph, The Book Barge and everything is as obvious as the black of his paint and the white of my milk. I sit very, very still like this, my head clear as day. 'Maybe we're finally growing up,' I whisper to Joseph when I'm in bed. 'Maybe we're getting wise.' On Sunday it'll be two years since the opening of the shop.

18

THAMES

This is the bit in the story when I go to London and make my fortune, because the towpaths there are paved with gold. I am well versed in the tale of Dick Whittington and his cat. I know the legend is based on the life of a man named Richard Whittington, a wealthy merchant and philanthropist, and that there is no historical evidence he had a rat-catching kitty who caught the eye of the King of Barbary. Instead, the improbable feline thread running through that story is believed to stem from the type of boat Whittington used for trading, which was known as a 'cat'. So far, so good. We can tick off the boat and even the trading. So as to manage expectations, however, it's fair to reveal now that I don't become Lord Mayor.

South of Oxford it's the Thames all the way down. The one really excellent thing about this river is that the locks are all manned. The flip side is you pay for little luxuries like these on the wide, wide water — there's a licence fee entirely separate from the £800-odd I'm paying British Waterways annually. Discovering how much a registration plate costs for the period I'm after (just over a month) makes my face do strange things. My jaw springs open and my eyes show a lot of white. I don't have that money. I hand over all the notes I *do* have and the lock keeper calculates this will keep me in river for the next couple of days and I figure that'll have to do until I think of something. By the time I stop for the next lock, I have. I add a very small head on the rotund '0' of the expiration date in matching blue marker pen. This gives me eight more days. It means I have to practise very elaborate distraction tactics every time the river authorities look at it too closely in the window. Like casually splashing big books overboard then theorising loudly about the accidental migrations of bottlenose whales. Or I'll try to smile winningly or ask if they want to see the rope burns on my hands. These are all small prices to pay.

I wouldn't normally use a bottlenose whale's name in vain like that. I'm one of the people who remember when one did, in fact, lumber upstream. It happened in the winter of 2006 when I was working in London as a journalist. The whale swam up by mistake, is, I think, what happened. It swam right past the Thames barrier, pulling people out of their offices and off buses and trains to take a look. But when it saw those schools of eyes blinking hard from the bank, the whale's own eyes filled with tears. Maybe the whale had heard that the city was phosphorescent. That it shone light because its buildings were tall enough to scrape the sun. But what it saw was only brown water and a thousand eyes. And this was like every other place in his oceans. At this the whale felt sad and she bled for the false city. Its people got upset at the sight. They demanded a barge pick her up and make her feel better about London, their town. But she shuddered at this and died on the spot in the same paroxysm. For a long time after I thought hard about the whale. I thought of how happy we all were when she was in our river and how this wasn't enough to keep her alive. Sometimes, when night dropped, I would look out across London and think, if only you'd waited. Here is the city twinkling as you were told. It was a matter of time. And then I resolved that all of London would be happier if there were always whales. And these whales would stay to play with our flashbulbs and curiosity if it was always sparkling night. These are very hard policies to put into action, however. And so I defer my mayoral candidacy until such time is right that I have whales spare and can

90

manipulate Greenwich Mean Time.

Although the Thames disappointed the bottlenose, there is much in the same river that delights me. I can go fast — much faster than on a canal — and this suits me because the bookshop has been hired for an event at Camden Locks at 6 p.m. on Friday. I left Oxford on Monday so I'm putting in five ten-hour days to get there. To begin with I waste a lot of time doing 360-degree turns for the hell of it and wherever I like. There's not much opportunity for this on the canals with a sixty-foot boat. Also, I discover the lock keepers only keep business hours, which I don't have enough of in this week. When they go home a big 'self service' sign gets hung on the gate and that means operating it yourself. This should be fine with all the practice I've had but these locks are different because they're electric and enormous. First time it takes about forty minutes of standing glumly at a panel that looks like a game console, randomly poking buttons through the pulled-down cuff of my anorak, to figure out the correct sequence. Rain swings down. When I finally get it right the boat kicks out into the middle of the lock with the plugholing water and I have to sprint to the other side and burn my palms again holding it in on the middle rope.

There are other mistakes I make. I run aground a lot by straying too near the banks of all the little islands. Called 'eyots' or 'aits', they're marked like code on my map in so many dashes and dots. Sometimes I run aground on the river bank too. Specifically, when I ignore a 'no mooring' sign in Abingdon and tie up to the railings opposite a pub. I rush in to use their toilet. When I rejoin the boat it stubbornly refuses to fight the current wiping its nose and instead turns with it into a sandbank. Barge poles, bow thrusters, reverse gear and various combinations of the three won't budge us. I sit on the roof swigging wine and pondering my options. Schoolchildren gather on the near pavement to mock. A horsey woman puts her hands around the corners of her mouth and unhelpfully sirens: 'Excuse me, lady on the river, but I think you may have run aground.' Another narrow boat eventually passes and tows me off with ropes.

19

FATHERS (part i)

There are so many big houses along the path of the Thames that I inevitably start thinking of the ones you crayon as a kid. Not the box/triangle architecture of your early primary years. I'm talking the mansions you aspire to as an eleven-year-old child of the capitalist 80s brought up watching *Annie* the musical. All you want is a palace and your parents to die so a Daddy Warbucks figure can fortuitously bridge the two.

It's been a long time since I've had the orphan hankering. Out here on the river, though, I feel pretty alone and so it starts floating in my head again. People often ask what I think about all day at the tiller for ten hours on my own and it's usually dumb stuff like this. I can be more precise: I'm wondering, if I was an orphan right now, who my new parents would be. Contextually, I think it would be nice if Old Father Thames was one. I've seen pictures of his statue at St John's Lock. They made it for the Great Exhibition in 1851 and he looks pretty paternal insofar as you can with just a loosely wrapped sheet covering your privates and a shovel swung jauntily to shoulder. He also looks pretty gay but I'm okay with that. Even aged eleven I think I saw the Warbucks/secretary coupling for the Hollywood sham it was. All his skipping and dancing and wanting a small boy in the first place, not Annie at all. If Papa Thames is the same way inclined, I decide Old Father Time might be a good match. Similar age. Same fondness for robes and flowing chin hair and for bearing gardening implements, although in this case a scythe. It could well turn out to be the Elton John/David Furnish relationship of the anthropomorphic world.

On the third day I wake up just south of Henley. Its annual boat race is a week away and chugging through the day before I saw grandstands being assembled and white marquees laid out flat next to them. I tied up between two trees where I could still watch the work going on into late evening. In the morning I'm woken by loud grunts outside. My first thought is that bears have caught a whiff of all my wasting cereal bars so I grab my bat in my sleeping bag and then keep really still. The grunts fade away for a while. I relax. Five minutes later though I can hear them again. By now I've dismissed the bear threat, obviously. This is rural Oxfordshire. I wonder instead if it's an enormous dog — the hound of Regattaville — humping one of the trees. This makes much more sense. I inch towards the bank window and twitch a curtain. Clear.

By now I'm pretty freaked out because the grunts are persisting at regular intervals. I try a window on the other side. Nothing. Oh, no wait . . . Ohhhh, SOMETHING! A sea of men! Waters of hot stuff! Little darts of testosterone flying by on boats! Scores of them! I've woken to race practice. Nay, to the runnels of heaven! I pull open the front door of the shop and stand, starkers from the waist up, taking deep gulps of their synchronised comehithers. Gorgeous river! Your breakfast beneficence knows no bounds. If I had any doubts about my new parentage, this incident allays all fears. Here is a spectacle only the kindest camp daddies could gift. I dress quickly and sit outside between the early shadows of them both, spooning custard straight from a carton. How happy this little family is! Time squeezes my shoulder. Thames tickles my feet. Boys row past all morning.

Maybe it's because I'm late leaving and consequently in a huge rush that, when I get to Cookham, I don't initially notice the two men arguing on the tall cruiser I share a lock with. I'm head down, hauling rope to keep from bruising their flash boat with the unpredictable steel fists of mine. When the lock empties, though, I'm surprised they let me exit first. Usually boats like theirs can't wait to breeze ahead. My engine phlegms to life and I head on out. I look back and laugh to see them muddled with plastic fenders and lines. It's rare that I get to feel superior about my boat-handling skills.

We keep meeting in locks after that. At Boulters Lock we exchange smiles and at Bray Lock I discover they've only just picked up their boat in Marlow. It cost £100,000 and they're taking it to St Catherine's Dock in London to rejoin their wives and toast their purchase. At Boveney Lock they get into difficulties again squeezing between a couple of other motor yachts. They confess they've never steered a boat and have already ripped the canopy off and scratched the side just leaving the marina where they bought her. They are very complimentary about my river progress, and I start warming to them. I insist they leave the lock ahead of me.

Following them through Windsor, however, I'm nervous to see them steer wide towards the smallest arch of the bridge ahead. It seems obvious from behind that their boat is too tall and they should be sticking to a middle course. I start screaming at them but they don't hear. As they near it though, they take up the screaming themselves and I see the water confused by their furious reversing. I laugh so hard my own boat prangs the side of the middle arch and the books inside somersault straight off the shelves and onto the floor. It's worse that evening when we all decide to moor. They keep throwing lines to me on the bank but their lousy aim and my bent-double giggles see me miss every one. Eventually, another girl comes out of the boat I'm tied by and catches it easy, even though she's holding a puppy in her other hand.

While I'm getting changed for the pub, one of the guys knocks on the hatch and asks if I've got an engineer's number. The boat won't turn off, he says. He's pretty wound up. I give him the digits of the sexy guy who fixed mine and feel pretty happy for the excuse to see him again. Before they can call him, though, I take a look myself. I can see where the keys pull out and, next to that, a big red STOP button. 'This is just a wild guess,' I tell them, finger over the obvious. They buy me dinner. For the rest of the trip to Teddington, where the river turns tidal, we stick together. They let me watch Wimbledon on their big plasma screen while we're waiting at locks.

We drink sparkling wine at every opportunity. I forget Fathers Thames and Time in all the bubbles and tennis. If they're hurt, they hide it well.

20

FATHERS (part ii)

My own dad joins me at Kingston-upon-Thames. Having him here allows me to recreate a little Dickensian scene that I love, but on the sly so he doesn't think I'm coming down with brain fever or something. He's astute to medical conditions like that because he's been a doctor all his life. My mum's a nurse. With their combined textbooks and anecdotes and the harrowing pictures of necrotising fasciitis in their surgical journals, I've grown up a mild hypochondriac. It's happening even now. The more I stand at the tiller worrying my dad will think I have brain fever, the more I fear I've actually developed it.

Brain fever is a dated term. It belongs in Victorian literature which, to be fair, is probably where I originally picked it up. I can't blame the *British Medical Journal* for everything. The diagnosis covers a range of potentially life-threatening illnesses and is usually linked to severe emotional shock. Nowadays we refer to the milder effects as post-traumatic stress disorder. In Dickens's day this was known as 'Railway Spine', in a nod to the high prevalence of train derailment survivors who suffered it. Dickens himself had first-hand experience. On 9th June 1865 he was almost killed in the Staplehurst disaster when the train he was travelling back from Paris in derailed on a viaduct in Kent. Physically unharmed, he rushed to the aid of fellow passengers with a flask of brandy and a hat full of water. In all, ten people died in the accident, some as Dickens was tending to them. Another forty were injured.

The event affected Dickens enormously. He lost his voice for two weeks and it stalled the engine of his furious writing. In the postscript of the novel he was working on at the time, he wrote: 'I can never be much nearer parting company with my readers for ever than I was then, until there shall be written against my life, the two words with which I have this day closed this book: — THE END.' The book was *Our Mutual Friend*. The very beginning is what I'm itching to perform.

The novel starts on the Thames, only slightly downstream from where we are now. There's 'a boat of dirty and disreputable appearance, with two figures in it'. He's 'a strong man with ragged grizzled hair'. She:

'sufficiently like him to be recognisable as his daughter.' He keeps his eyes fixed on the river. She watches his face just as keenly. But, Dickens writes, 'in the intensity of her look there was a touch of dread or horror'. They tow a dead body.

This is the expression I'm trying to achieve. I stare hard at my dad in the pastel light of dawn but he's pointing out the sights of Richmond or counting the aeroplanes that split the sky from night to new day. When I do catch his eye — my cheeks wan, chin jittery, one eyebrow raised *aghast* — he says I look hungry. 'Go inside,' he says, 'Mum's put some cereal bars in my bag for you.' He doesn't read me right.

I love *Our Mutual Friend* for all sorts of reasons, from the river that ribbons through to the hopeful theme of turning waste into true wealth. It's a book about rising from the dust heaps and from the brink of death. It's a polishing up and a cleaning off and a breathing new life into. You can see why it appeals to a failing, floating bookseller girl. And then there's the strange temper of the novel, the reluctance to be definitely one thing or absolutely another. The inbetween of it all. And that's also because of the way Dickens writes it — to deadline and often disjunctively. His imagination bolts in one bit.

And stops just as suddenly. It's both realistic and hallucinatory. It's lifelike, like that.

There's one other part of *Our Mutual Friend* that gets me thinking today. It's Dickens's obsession in it with ways of reading. There are two kinds that his characters display: one perfunctory, born of the classroom and rote, the other *performative*. Just as I try my Lizzie Hexham mask, so the nouveau-riche Boffin acts out the tales of all the misers he's read, to demonstrate the dangers of wealth. Reading, like all the best verbs, is a doing word, Dickens says.

More than that. I started reading relatively late. I only began school a few months shy of age six. Before then, my mother would sometimes take me with her to work. While she performed ultrasounds on pregnant women, I would play quietly in the room behind. She gave me old X-ray images alongside my bag of toys. With these dark sheets in hand, I learnt then to read black and white as a diagnostic tool. To fix things. To make a person better. Later, when I was taught to recognise a leaf of printed words, I knew the letter shapes as little bones that, when fused together correctly, could mend a person in all sorts of useful ways.

I have an overwhelming desire to share this with my dad right now. I don't want him to think I'm hungry out here, or cold, or unsatisfied, upset, or any other worrying thing. I want him to know I have ways of crutching and pinning like he does. I have a whole first-aid box of poems, short stories, strange bright pills of drama, sugared teaspoons of novel in there. I want him to know we're not so different. That I grew up watching him closely and read what he did in my own way. I want him to read *this* and say, 'You're doing fine, daughter.'

21

CAMDEN

Although I joked earlier about the Dick Whittington tale, I have great confidence that London will be good for my shop. It sort of *has* to be. I'm low on food, I need money for diesel and I need to pay off my wholesaler's bill so I can order more stock. I'm nervous about London at the same time, though. I lived here for a couple of years after graduating, in a small studio flat near Kings Cross. There was a fold-down bed and the click, click, click of prostitute's heels on the other side of the iron-barred window. I couldn't say I hated that time — there was so much I found exciting. But I couldn't say I was happy. I felt that the city expected things from me. I wanted to please it however I could. I tunnelled, lower even than the tricolour tube trains, and made another network of commutes and shift work, high rent, higher heels, confident acquaintances, playing cool, too bright smiles, time deficiency, escalators, not minding, not reading, not looking up, not looking down, never noticing the canal I crossed every day. I forgot where I was going to, so just stayed buzzing around on this line until I flew to Beijing on holiday and, in genuine surprise, looked out over the Summer Palace one bright November morning and noted that other places still exist.

Maybe London hasn't forgotten this small treachery. When I get to Camden there's nowhere to moor except in the way of trip boats. On my first day, in the middle of a kids' book signing, one operator storms in and gives me five minutes to move before he unties the ropes himself and drags me. I'm helped by a bystander who, by crazy coincidence, happens to be one of Narsh's friends. He tells me how, when Narsh was looking after things and I was pedalling Wales, one of their mates had been hospitalised because of my boat. He was kneeling down on the stern to loosen a rope and stabbed his head on the sharp point of the tiller pin getting up. 'There was blood everywhere,' he tells me. 'We thought he'd need surgery.' I ask him to keep his voice down. The kids and parents and author inside are all looking mutinous. We take the boat through the lock and moor illegally next to another one. People start skinning up on the stairs. A rap outfit rains expletives from the roof recording a music video. A shrill woman in white denim complains her jeans have been ruined by sitting on the weather-loosened fibres of my faux lawn. She points to her green-flocked arse, which looks like a Sylvanian Families tundra. I add NO HIP-HOP and NO SITTING ON THE LAWN to my growing list of shop rules, but choose to go easy on the weed. My bill of banned behaviour is already long enough:

HARD LIMITS
- I don't always want to be the go-to girl when you see a duck in distress. Sometimes you should just ring the RSPCA straight off.
- Don't try to climb through the window.
- Don't bang your head on the way out.
- Don't extol the virtues of price checker apps.
- Don't ask me my opening hours. Even I'm not privy to such information.
- Yes, you can take photos — but not when I inexplicably have biscuit crumbs in my eyelashes.
- Don't ask if you can take off your shoes. You can't. Feet smell.
- Don't question the dust.
- Never mind where I go to the loo.
- Don't all rush in on Boxing Day to tell me you got a Kindle for Christmas and it's great.

- Definitely don't ask if I want to 'check out all the free books on it by borrowing it until Epiphany.'
- Being narrow is a distinguishing feature of most canal boats. Don't feel any special need to comment on it.
- I'd rather you paid in Victoria sponge than Scottish notes — and that's not a xenophobic thing.
- Yes, I knitted those bookmarks myself before you start slagging them off.
- Don't cry.
- Don't stare at me if I'm crying.
- I'm a bit precious about the bin. Please throw your rubbish away outside unless it's 'clean' rubbish. I dunno, like a sheaf of paper. Or fabric. Anything else, outside. Please don't ask to throw rubbish away. It makes me extremely uncomfortable as I feel pressured to say yes but inside I'm screaming, 'No! Dirty! Get it away from near my ankles!'
- Children, don't ask where the 'on' button is on the typewriters. This just makes me feel old.
- Children, don't sit on the typewriters either.
- Kids, just leave the typewriters alone, OK?
- Please don't fart. This bookshop is very

small and quite poorly ventilated. I've thrown perpetrators out before now.

- Don't ask if it's a bookshop.
- Don't say: 'I've got so many books at home I could probably open my own bookshop.'
- 'I have no children to leave it to in my will' is probably the worst excuse for not buying a £7.99 paperback. Don't use it.
- Please, strangers in my bookshop, don't feel the need to divulge any details of your marital problems or sexual deviances. Showing a shop girl a nudie picture on your mobile phone of the woman you're cheating on your wife with is a bit awkward.
- Don't brand me an ungrateful pacifist for not carrying books on weaponry or battlefields.
- To the young man whose first words upon entering the shop were: 'I know I look like Saddam Hussein
- but don't get scared, I'm not . . . ' DON'T YOU KNOW a) HE'S DEAD b) HE HAD A THICKER MOUSTACHE?!

When I close up for the day, about 9 p.m., I notice there's a pigeon on the path outside with people standing around and pointing at him with a twig. I go out to see what's happening. The bird's on his belly, his open beak making a less-than sign he's dying. Someone wants to throw him in the canal to put him out of his misery. A couple of teenage girls are saying he should be stamped on because he's dirty. I'm suddenly furious with them all, how they're hawking around him. I pick him up and take him round to the front of the boat, lay him in the dead grass of one of my plant tubs. I'm embarrassed about doing it and what the people standing there think of me, but I'm angry more than anything. I had a pigeon once and I had dreams for us. I'll tell you about it next.

In the morning there is piss and vomit all over my Astroturf lawn. And in the tub of dead grass is a lifeless pigeon, one wet wing outstretched. Gertrude Stein formerly wrote about pigeons on the grass. 'Pigeons on the grass alas. / Pigeons on the grass alas,' is the repetitive, illogical gist of that work.

22

PIGEON

I had a pigeon once and I had dreams for us. His name was Nelson, after the Admiral Lord, because when I found him, he could use just one arm. Nelson was a racing pigeon from Bristol that, for unknown reasons, ended up staring down traffic on a narrow lane near the flat I used to share with Stu. Stu was dropping me off at the shop for the monthly book club I run when we were forced to swerve past him. He didn't blink. 'If he's still there on the way back', I said, 'let's pick him up.' Three hours later our car headlights made out his pedestrian colours for the second time. He was as we left him — upright, stationary, wide-eyed in the wash of main beams. But we noticed this time that his left wing hung like a drawn curtain and he didn't struggle when we picked him up and rested him in an empty book box from my wholesaler.

When we got him in the house we opened the cardboard sides for a proper look. He had soiled the paper and waded around in it so his claws had milky-green tide marks. We gave him sugared water and rang the number on his ring. The man said, 'I can arrange repatriation on Monday but if his wing's broken he's no good to me any more, if you see what I mean.' I hung up and told Stu that our pigeon's owner was a Nazi. I drove back to my parents' that night, Nelson boxed on the passenger seat, and sang him love songs from the radio.

The next day I took him to the vet in a pink plastic cat basket. 'I think his wing's broken,' I said.

'I'll take him out the back and have one of the nurses euthanise him later,' the vet said. I blinked quickly.

'You're going to kill him too? You haven't even *glanced* at him!' So the vet gave a withering smile and picked Nelson up and stretched out the damaged wing and coughed and shook his head and then made this weird analogy:

An injured pigeon is like a wounded soldier. By all means send them home in army helicopters, shovel their crudely amputated limbs into freezer bags and pop those aboard too. Our war hero will spend at least six months recovering. Doctors will reattach his legs and arms and stitch closed his spilling innards. He'll slowly, painfully, learn how to speak again and use a fork and get back on his feet. His nightmares may subside, his disfigured face will become more familiar in the mirror. Then the army will send him back to Afghanistan and he'll be blown up into a thousand bloodied pieces when he limps over an IED on his first day in action. And all that surgery will have been for nothing.

Nelson and I looked at each other and at the vet and then back at each other. The vet looked at the clock. 'If it's okay with you', I mumbled, 'I'll take him home. There are a couple of cats around my parents' garden but it's hardly Helmand Province. I think he'll be okay. He's a bird of peace. A conscientious objector.' The vet shrugged and washed his hands at the sink.

'As a special favour', he turned to wink, 'I won't charge you for this consultation.'

So Nelson and I returned home via a pet shop to pick out a medium-sized rabbit hutch and some seed. I decorated the walls with photos of me holding an eagle on a glove, which one of my weird customers who's a falconer took the summer previously. I think, once Nelson got over the initial bird of prey distress, he appreciated these little touches that reassured him I am a friend of all bird life. In return, he taught me everything he knew about his species. I was particularly curious about his unclosing eyes. Sometimes I'd spy on him from the kitchen window to see if he'd let his guard — and lid — slip. He never did. 'Pigeon eyes', he told me, 'are remarkable. They have a 340-degree field of vision.' I surmised from this that my kitchen surveillance may not have been as covert as I'd hoped.

Nelson slept in his hutch at night but had freedom of the lawn by day. Every morning he'd make a neat dismount from the wooden perch and hurry out into the middle of the grass to stretch his wings. Both arms outstretched, he'd beat the air as if thwarting crucifixion. He never took off. One morning my mother suggested providing height might help his flight efforts. We put him on the branch of a tree. Nelson stayed in his crow's nest for many hours. He looked askance at the dog, who was gnawing a tennis ball, and at my mother, who was hanging sheets on the washing line. He saved his most severe look for me, who was logging every incidence of pigeons as they appear in literature. There is a reference in Shakespeare's *As You Like It* and in Dickens' *Barnaby Rudge*. Patrick Suskind and Isaac Bashevis Singer wrote a pigeon novella and short story respectively. They provide moral instruction in *Aesop's Fables* and a means of escape for Cornelius van Baerle in Dumas's *The Black Tulip*. When Nelson finally found courage and first fell, then scrambled his wings to pound the distance to the pitched roof, I thought that only one writer has captured pigeons as correctly on page as mine now looked on the red tiles. In his four-line poem, *Pigeons*, Vikram Seth describes them 'Flaunting, against their civic coats, / The glossy oils that scarf their throats.'

With Nelson recovered, I now made enthusiastic plans for him to accompany me on The Book Barge's impending voyage. I saw him as the shop's harbinger in every town and village, swooping ahead with the message of new books and free tea clutched between his dinosaur fingers. I'll take him to London, I promised, on a pilgrimage to his columned namesake in Trafalgar Square. Here he'd become a political icon, I envisaged. We'd hold banners protesting the 2007 ban on the feeding of pigeons in what has become their Mecca and their playground. And after that we'd chug out of the city and back to the fields. He'd run on the wind and tap dance on my shoulder. He'd bowsprit and bring down the sun. He'd be a companion.

A week before leaving, Nelson wasn't waiting in his hutch when I came back from work. I walked around the garden shaking the seed in his bowl and scanning the rooftop and fence for the grey uniform of the Bristol Luftwaffe that he still wore. Only when I saw the bloodbath by the front gate did I know that the vet's bleak prophecy had come true.

23

CORNFLOUR

When the pigeon in Camden dies on me too, I interpret it as a sign. Obviously, it's a sign that I'm not very proficient at caring for birds. But it's also a sign of something bigger. When the second pigeon dies I'm not upset. I react very differently.

I already mentioned a book I was reading before starting this trip, about the power of everyday boredom. I don't feel bored now so much as overwhelmed by the realisation that the boredom has gone. I mean, it's probably still there, but not as a separate thing. It's like a thickening agent you add to food — it doesn't change the taste and you don't necessarily know it's there except that it makes everything stronger. It's kitchen chemistry, nothing fancier than that, but it can do amazing things. I've seen the experiment where you add cornflour to water and then jump on it. The molecules lock together and can take a person's weight. After the pressure is released it returns to a liquid state. I even know the name for this beefed-up juice — it's called a non-Newtonian fluid. Exactly a year earlier I read a piece on the BBC website about how similar science is being manipulated by the military to create a new kind of body armour. The article described a 'bullet-proof custard'. When the second pigeon dies I feel strengthened in the same way. Leaving the bird carcass on the front of the boat, exactly how I found it when I got up, I head to Kings Cross.

The plan is quite simple — I'll moor outside the *Guardian* newspaper's headquarters there and stay put until they take notice and commend the shop to print. To date, probably only a couple of hundred people know that The Book Barge exists and how much I want it to stay open. Although the trip has gone some way towards boosting that number, Twitter and Facebook followers remain stubbornly below the 100 mark and, being my primary method of sharing where I am and what I need, it's imperative to drive this number up if there's any hope of lasting the whole six months. National press could make a real difference. Short of self-immolation on a pyre of Kindles, I am running out of other ideas.

Maybe it's this stench of desperation that alerts the security guard to my arrival. I've only been moored five minutes — barely time to dry shampoo my socks or slide a roll-on over last night's sweating dinner plate — before I hear his knock. The walkie-talkie in his hand utters strange pleasantries but the man himself makes no greeting. He looks up and down the boat and bends stiffly to peer through a window. Nervous, I glove one of my hands with the brown sock I'm still holding. The hairspray has left creamy chalk marks over it so now my whole arm looks like an over-sized shiitake mushroom and I can see this doesn't go unnoticed by the guard. We go through the whole rigmarole of mooring permissions and I'm surprised to learn that this side of the canal is deemed private property. Seeing as the British Waterways contacts I've memorised won't hold sway here, I switch to a roll call of *Guardian* books department journalists instead, which the man duly notes on a small pad. In the morning he'll verify my information, he says, but for now I must leave immediately. He sniffs the air ill-temperedly.

I spend the following days in furious activity in the space directly opposite. I sponge the Camden urine from the gunwales and peel dried upchuck from the Astroturf. My mum comes down with Pledge and Windolene and I finally eject the spider commune, which has been making free love and silky ban-the-bomb signs behind the Beatrix Potter set since October 2009. I max my remaining wholesaler credit on a modest delivery of prize-winning new fiction and open new accounts direct with publishers to top up the shelves still more. I bury the invoices in my handbag and my head behind a column of boxes hauling all these books across London on the blue-in-the-face Piccadilly line. Finally, I sit down to write a new blog.

These posts, which I try to update twice weekly, have been getting increasingly maudlin. They follow the basic narrative of failed relationships. I play the wheedling suitor in the early days of the voyage, coaxing customers with compliments on their towns and reading tastes. Later posts, however, show lack of effort and lazy habits. I'm here, they say, but don't hope for any more than that. The monosyllables creep in. The 'too tired' excuse comes out to explain my longer silences. One day, too late, I realise what I've lost. These blogs echo the drunk diallings of a desperate ex-girlfriend. *I'll do anything*, they promise. *You wanna shake things up under the cover price? Strip my assets. Spank my bottom line. I'll give you 3-for-2 stickers — with nipple tassels on.* I have no shame. I have plumbed the depths of the Regents Canal at Brentford.

But when you hit bottom, the only way is up. I look in the mirrored windows of the offices across the water and take a deep breath. Write about what you know, those busy bent heads behind them would nod. Write to make you strong. *Hello folks*, I begin and I can feel the breezy lines are back again. *Let me tell you an easy way to remove three-day-old retch from the green carpeted roof of your local floating bookshop. The secret, I'll divulge, is to add a little something to help it gelatinise . . .*

24

MICAWBER

It sounds too convenient to say that after this things were different. They really were though. The same day a delegation from the *Guardian* books department comes over and buys stuff, records a podcast and pays lovely compliments. They don't even seem to mind I plundered their names attempting to manipulate mooring regulations — or are perhaps too polite to bring it up. Then *The Evening Standard* runs a piece and *The Express* follows suit. A journalist from *The Independent* calls to see if I'd like to use his shower, takes me to a house party after, and then puts a piece in the paper punnily entitled 'How to Stay Afloat as a Bookseller'. When I head down the canal towards Hackney, I have the good fortune of Erica Wagner, *Times* Literary Editor, jogging past. She later writes that 'all life is aboard The Book Barge', even though by this time I've removed the rotting pigeon cadaver — and the maggots within. She adds that mine is the only literary blog she's read offering such pertinent advice on the disinfection of puke. Or words to that effect. Something for my parents to be proud of.

Overnight the Twitter count shoots up to 2,000 and my inbox starts screaming like Tippi Hedren on the film poster for *The Birds* because there are so many messages winging in. Mostly they're food and bed offers but a few authors also get in touch to do free readings and I'm especially grateful for these. There's a lot of plain weird stuff too. A guy in Australia plots a course to bring the boat to Brisbane. He schedules a five-day stopover on a Thai island, acknowledging 'you'll probably be pretty tired if you're making this trip single-handed'. He has me hugging the coast as often as is practical, and I reply telling him I appreciate this concession because the big wide sea is not something my boat particularly relishes the prospect of. I tell him the law books he's requested I carry with me are currently out of stock.

Other beneficences include six months of free cuppas courtesy of a tea company, who hand-deliver boxes of their herbal infusions while I'm moored in Haggerston. I also have an engine problem fixed free of charge that has been bothering me since Warwickshire. For the first time I'm able to write out lengthy shopping lists, hand this to a customer, and exchange books to the value of the till receipt and bagged groceries they return later that day. Ocado suddenly seems comparatively caveman. Victoria sponge cakes, which I let slip are my favourite, tier daily on my desk. They prove useful lock-shirking collateral. Channelling Lady Justice, I learn to carry a plate in one hand, a windlass in another, and blindly mete out both to the first runner that crosses my towpath. That analogy isn't an idle one. For the first time since opening the shop I feel a strange sense of both reprieve and vindication — that I've narrowly escaped something terrible (a punishment I probably deserved for my business mismanagements) but that I've also been proved right for persisting. It's a giddy, light feeling. I don't know how long it will last so I hold its hand tight while I can.

When a couple called Richard and Amy come aboard in Angel, the coincidence of the address they scribble down in return for a kids' book — *The Itch of the Golden Nit* — makes me squeeze that hand even harder. They live on Micawber Street, named after the impoverished *David Copperfield* character who exists in the hopeful expectation that 'something will turn up'. Here, at last, it has. I visit for lunch and bathroom facilities the very next day and delight further to discover the building is a former British Library book repository, currently being managed by a live-in guardian scheme whereby tenants pay substantially reduced rent to occupy empty buildings (usually big office or warehouse ones) until developers are ready to begin their projects. In a city like London, where inflated living costs can see residents fork out over £1,000 a month for a one-bed flat rental, paying just 10 per cent for a grand-proportioned room, communal kitchen and free studio space downstairs seems remarkable. In its frugality it also neatly fits the so-called Micawber Principle, based on his reflection: 'Annual income twenty pounds, annual expenditure nineteen pounds nineteen and six, result happiness. Annual income twenty pounds, annual expenditure twenty pounds ought and six, result misery.' This is economics I can understand. Interestingly, the site is later transformed into a swanky six-storey apartment building called Folio, complete with gym. Estate agent details hint at 'stylish interiors', 'metropolitan living' and an abundance of balconies. Price on application, of course. I worry for Micawber's Principle.

Later that day I take the boat back through the Islington Tunnel to Kings Cross with the author Lee Rourke, who wrote the book about boredom, *The Canal*. We had arranged that he'd do a reading and signing but me, him, the people who have come along for the event, we're mostly just getting spooked by the 960 yards of darkness and the dripping. I want to tell Lee things about his book but I'm too shy, even though it's black enough to avoid seeing his reaction if I say something really dumb. What I want to say is this: thank you. It's what I like to say when I close most books. Sometimes it's just polite — I enjoyed reading the story, it entertained me. But sometimes there's much more invested in those two words. Sometimes I feel like I owe the book — and in that case thank you seems the very least I can say. This is the case with *The Canal*. I can draw a direct line from reading it to being here now. I appreciate that, I want to say.

For the rest of July and most of August I go backwards and forwards with my bookshop between the *Guardian* building at Kings Cross and the bottom of Broadway Market in Hackney. Lee Rourke writes a newspaper article about it. The piece is titled 'A Bookshop Going Places'.

25

ACQUISI-TEARS

On one of these journeys a man wearing Christ-like hair and double linen thumbs a lift. He is a guru, he tells me, dragging a deckchair from inside over to where I stand at the tiller. And he is also an author. The man's name is The Acquisitor. So-called, he says, because he loves lucre. It's difficult to hear properly over the growl of the engine and I initially mistake him for a Lycra lover instead. I am swiftly corrected and have to agree he does not look like a man who favours clinging textiles. We discuss the pros of hemp-spun vestments for several minutes.

The Acquisitor is an unusual sort of person. This comes as some surprise as I'd recently reached the satisfying conclusion I'd seen it all when passing a blue, full-bodied spandex-catsuited creature, with captain's hat, steering a narrow boat further north. The Acquisitor, though less startlingly coutured, has the eccentric edge because he promises to galvanise me to Greatness. I did not cap up that 'g', by the way. He did. I warn him this is a mighty ask but admit I have every confidence in his abilities because, by this point, I am privy to A Brief History of The Acquisitor (and Some of his Online Videos).

A Brief History of The Acquisitor

The Acquisitor is a self-styled 'nomad, potter and profit prophet'. He likes 'nurturing mankind's potential' just as much as he enjoys 'glazing vases and other clay vessels in far-flung corners of the globe'. He has unlocked the secrets of 'WEALTH and POPULARITY' and he can give the key to 'YOU' too if you invest in his extensively researched tome Winsome and Worth a Million.

The Acquisitor is also fluent in 'Future Whispering', which allows its proponents to 'Favourably Alter their Fate'. Learn how to 'Have a Conversation with Destiny'. All the essential vocab is contained on a very reasonably priced audio CD.

To summarise, The Acquisitor knows that everyone is capable of 'Sculpting their Own Success'. If you are short of 'WEALTH' or 'POPULARITY' and want to try before you buy his backlist, 'YOU', like me, can watch Some of his Online Videos instead. My favourite is the 'ACQUISI-TEARS Challenge' and this is what it looks like:

The *ACQUISI-TEARS* Challenge

The Acquisitor has been very blessed to study 'THANKFULNESS' and believes we have a lot to be thankful for.

I don't disagree. In fact, in the previous chapter I think you'll find I admit even to lavishing loud praise on the endpapers of my reading material. Where The Acquisitor shows his superior grasp of 'THANKFULNESS' is in the *method* in his madness. The Acquisitor has compiled a *'PRAISE BE!* POCKET BOOK'. In it he writes down all the things he is grateful for, because this is what makes us 'GREAT'. Get it? The Acquisitor suggests that even when we're standing in a really long queue, maybe at Caffé Nero or the cash machine or the oncology department, if we pull out our own *Praise Be!* Pocket Book and read just a few entries we'll feel immediately better about the world, and possibly even great about things again.

To help me compile my *Praise Be!* Pocket Book, The Acquisitor suggests I go through the alphabet for prompts. A could be for Avocado, he explains, B is for Beautiful

Babies, which he appreciates just as much. He is also thankful for Cats — his C word. Unfortunately he has to skip D because he can't think of anything, but he gets back on track with E. E is for Ears. The Acquisitor explains that I'm using my Ears right now to hear his message. This is something to be grateful for, is the insinuation. There are lots more examples The Acquisitor gives me, including being thankful that I woke up this morning. Many people simply don't, he tells me. I get the impression that we're close to scraping the barrel by this point so divert his attention to a moorhen dragging its foot in a knotted plastic bag on the other side of the canal. I am grateful for that moorhen as much as I am sorry for its predicament.

Before he leaves, The Acquisitor sets me the challenge. Every morning I must write down three things that I'm grateful for. I must do this for the next forty days. By the time forty days is up, The Acquisitor is confident that I'll have broken down in acquisi-tears. Even though this sounds like the symptom of some kind of nervous collapse, The Acquisitor assures me that, on the contrary, these will be tears of joy! It's a beautiful thing! It's a *transcendent* thing! I did not add those exclamation marks. Again, he did. Looking at The Acquisitor with his shining teeth and very healthy hair, I want to warn him that I don't have much staying power and that forty days seems an awful long time. And must the list always be updated in the mornings, I should find out, for I hate the mornings. When I wake up, I want to die. I usually think: I wish I'd passed in the night and never seen this day, whose sunlight punches me in the face.

But I tell The Acquisitor nothing for at that moment he asks if we can consensually hug. I let the jaw of his flaxen shirt arms close around me and his hands champ up and down my spine. It feels like a very practised movement and, in comparison, my reciprocal hug is stiff and awkward. I worry he can hear that I am counting to forty in my head instead of feeling stuff. Afterwards, when The Acquisitor has let go, I say: 'Wow, you're a really good hugger.' And that's how I end up in a second clutch.

26

MONTAIGNE

All that The Acquisitor has told me I stuff away to digest later. In fact, I pick over it the very next morning on my way to The Wellcome Library, which houses an impressive medical history collection and is where my sister-in-law Christy works. I've been meeting her here semi-regularly while the boat's been in London because she buys me breakfast in the canteen and, afterwards, lends me her security pass so I can use the showers on the top floor. The top floor is a conference facility so is nearly always empty at 8 a.m. The bathrooms are big and each has a toilet, washbasin and clothes hanger on one side, and an enormous shower behind the partition wall on the other. The first day I used it I discovered the lights are on a timer. If you spend too long under the shower without walking back into the toilet area and jumping around a little under the sensor you're plunged into darkness and likely to smack your elbow on the tap, as I did in a panic for my clothes. Once you remember

131

this, however, you can spend upwards of an hour in there, light bulbs burning bright the whole time, and shave your armpits and floss your teeth and pluck your eyebrows too.

Everything considered, it's definitely something to put in the *Praise Be!* Pocket Book. I'm walking down the Euston Road to Christy now and I can think of a second thing straight off because they're giving me a blister: my new shoes. I swapped them for books about a week ago because my other ballet pumps had holes in the sole from where the engine heat of the boat slowly melts the rubber when I'm wearing them at the tiller. These new ones are a size too small, but I'm still chuffed because it's not everyday you can persuade a stranger to shoe you in return for two kids' picture books. These are right up there with my Hugo Boss Orange perfume coup. They hurt like hell though, especially sidestepping out of the path of the 73 bus to Stoke Newington when I cross the road by Pizza Express.

Christy's not in a great rush for her pass back this morning as her meeting has been cancelled. Take a long shower, she says, and come find me back at my desk when you're done. I add Christy to my things-to-be-thankful for list. She's not just generous with her swipe card, she's super-clever too. She works on the Wellcome Library's digitisation project but mainly she's smart in how she handles my brother. Like this breakfast-at-work thing: she's doing it to avoid his weird barbecue diet, which he's trialling at every meal for the entire month of July. It's not such a big deal when you know my brother's eating habits. He doesn't generally touch anything that grows on a tree or in the ground. He figures he eats so many creatures that consume this green, healthy stuff themselves that he'll get it secondhand anyway. Other than that, it's pretty much just Custard Creams and Galaxy Minstrels that provide any non-carnivorous variety. I'm presuming what he means by the barbecue diet is that he's trying to cut out this confectionery crap. Or maybe amalgamate them into the lamb burgers as toppings so he can pretend to be skipping pudding. Either way, he's spooning cold kebab from a breakfast bowl at 7.30 a.m. every morning and Christy has the foresight to realise leaving the house on an empty stomach is more palatable than witnessing this.

Up on the top floor I stroll around a while and admire the views. There are chairs laid out up there today and a table of refreshments, but I don't think anything of it and take my shower as usual. Because I've got a little extra time, I clip my toenails to try and make more space in the shoes. I also shave my legs so I can put on the hot pants I've carried, unworn, since leaving home. I sing while I'm doing this. I do heavy star jumps under the sensor between legs to keep the light aware that I'm still around. When I'm finished, I remember the chairs outside and think how nice it'd be to pull one up to a big window in the corner and watch the buses below beetling by while my hair dries. I've bought a book in the shop downstairs by a former Wellcome Library employee, a woman called Sarah Bakewell, so I could read that too. It's a biography of the French Renaissance essayist Michel de Montaigne and is called *How to Live*. I'm curious to find whether the advice contained makes any mention of acquisi-tears. Piling my hair into a pink towel turban I get dressed into short shorts and panda-motif T-shirt, leaving my too-tight shoes in my bag for a little while longer, and I step out.

It's the woman on the front row I see first. Her own eyes widen and play with the discomfort that's souring my mouth. She raises a hand across the lower half of her face and makes a catty comment behind it, which the grey-suited man to her right finds funny.

A few other people are giggling quietly on the rows behind but the man who's presenting hasn't noticed and goes on talking about whatever the seminar's supposed to be on. I immediately pull the towel from my head and stuff it in my bag. My hair tangles on my shoulders making dark epaulettes of water. I look down to my bare feet so that it falls forward around my face instead, hot under all their stares.

When I finally get round to reading about Montaigne many months later, a comment he made about his library makes me think of that humiliating moment in the Wellcome one. Montaigne retired from public life in 1571, aged just thirty-eight, to be among his books. He wrote: 'Sorry the man, to my mind, who has not in his own home a place to be all by himself, to pay his court privately to himself, *to hide.*'

27

SATURDAY

The last Saturday I spend in London I remember as the best of my trip. I take the boat from Angel to Broadway Market early and tie it to the railings on the other side of Acton's Lock. The last time I moored here the water was clear to the junk-strewn bottom. People had used the roof of the boat as a diving board into it at 5 a.m. one morning. The light had only just begun stippling the water so the scene had a hesitant charm, even though the boys were laughing and splashing loud enough to make some of the curtains in the flats opposite twitch. I could hear at least two people still on the roof. The bottles they were drinking from rang the boat like a tuning fork every time they were put down. It felt like we were all vibrating together. I felt part of their joy, even half intoxicated by sleep and behind the thin glass.

This time though, the water is veiled by green weed. The boat has been splitting through it all morning because it trails as far back as the Islington tunnel. Now that I'm moored and the engine is still, the weed sidles back over. I close up to clean my teeth in one of the delis that bank the market and to look at the undressed trestles that will become stalls.

There's a book signing on the boat from 10 a.m. but it's busy well before then. People just keep coming in and buying stuff and being interested. I can hear the author/illustrator out the front reading aloud to some toddlers. 'Billy hated toothbrushes,' her story goes. 'He had tried them all.' The people inside the boat are talking about other books and reading in their heads, or bits aloud, or asking me how the bookshop came about. There's this steady hum of chatter and pages and people clicking photographs on their mobile phones and, to me, it sounds orchestral. I'm so scared of conducting it wrong but they're not even looking, they just keep playing their parts like today has been rehearsed a thousand times. I seem the only one who knows different.

At lunch I leave the shop to a customer while I run back to the market to use a bathroom. All the hip, young people look like so many bees nosing pistils behind the bright tarpaulin of those pop-up stores. I want to be with them, picking through the crockery piles and clothes hangers. I want to be them. I take about half an hour out in total just wandering round, head still buzzing, touching little bits of jewellery and pretty dresses that twist in the breeze.

For a couple of hours in the afternoon I have a 'Two Bookshops for the Price of One' event with Wood Green's Big Green Bookshop. Simon from their store has come down to use the back quarter of the boat for his books, while I keep the rest as my shop. Big Green Bookshop has been pretty inspirational to me. It opened a year before mine and in the same vein of excited naïveté: 'Open a bookshop, what could possibly go wrong?' Except, of course, its owners have over thirty-five years of experience between them and I had none. Despite this, they've always been unreservedly supportive on Twitter and now in person. Their stock selection, huge range of events and the flapjacks they dish out at their under-fives stories and songs session are the benchmark. Having them on board, *literally*, like this feels momentous. I remember a few years ago when Stu took me to his local team, Chasetown, playing Oldham in a cold November FA Cup first-round home tie. We saw them rubbing their hands and blowing on them too before the whistle shouted to start. In those

138

automatic gestures was all the glee — and supplication — of sharing a field with pros. I feel the same. And, in the background maybe, some vague health and safety concerns about the exceptional crowd numbers.

The whiteboard above the desk is scribbled hard today, greedy from all the success I've had recently. As well as the usual, I've requested a quiche and a haircut. Mine, though washed, is looking wispy at the ends and shapeless. It could do with a trim and I've Facebooked this fact extensively, expecting a Toni & Guy-type salon to follow the tea company's suit and offer pro bono services in return for free publicity. Instead, at around 5 p.m. when I'm thinking of closing up, a Slovenian woman walks into the shop and, after a couple of minutes browsing, approaches the desk with a copy of *Beside the Sea* by Veronique Olmi. Then she asks to borrow my yellow-handled paper scissors. When I put two and two together I'm inclined to give her the book for free rather than have her hacking at my hair with desk stationery. But the journalist from the *Independent* is back in the shop and quite a few other customers are looking over, curious, with cameras, so I sigh and go with it. I fetch the towel from the cupboard to cover my clothes and pass the scissors, metal first. The journalist watches keenly for a couple of minutes and then looks uncomfortable. He picks up the guitar he brought down and breaks into a rendition of Rolling Stones *You Can't Always Get What You Want*. This isn't helping much. My hair's quite long and I like it this way. I've been going to the same hairdresser since I was fifteen and I like *this* too. Basically, when it comes to hair I'm a creature of half-headed highlights and one-inch trim habit. I like chewing my ends when I'm on the phone and the conversation's crap. I like shaking it out of the pistachio and brown leather Vespa motorbike helmet I have at home, even though I don't ever ride a motorbike. I like pretending it really is hair like a wheat field that Paul Weller would run through. I like tugging at it when boys make me nervous. I like tucking it behind my ears before I eat. What I don't like though, is the look of the lengths that are falling to the floor around my black swivel desk chair.

When she's finished I get out a mirror. Even though I want to cry, I compliment the severe styling and ask where she works if I want to come back in a few months. 'Oh, I'm not a *hairdresser*,' she exclaims, seeming to take mild offence. 'I work as a psychotherapist. I've never cut someone's hair before.' She walks off the boat whistling, taking her book of infanticidal French motherhood with her. I shoo everyone out of the shop soon after and sit dejectedly at the desk, feet still encircled by my shorn locks. 'Mirror, mirror in the bookstore, who's the fuck-wittedest of them all?' I ask the looking glass. 'Why you are,' the face smirks back. I don't have time to grieve, however. There's a knock on the hatch and a photographer from a London magazine, whose appointment I had forgotten. His name is Tom. 'Tom,' I say, 'look at my hair. It's all gone.'

That night I go for a drink with Tom. First we walk up to the gate of Acton's Lock and sit there with the Portuguese students, sharing their red wine from my plastic cups. With all the green weed and the sky still blue it's pretty as a picture here and maybe Tom thinks so too because he's at his camera all the time. Some moments it's all set so right I forget we're just kicking our feet over a lock. How we're all grouped and powdered by the white spray forcing the gate, it feels like drawing-room design, with the chamber we peer into papered elegant William Morris.

We meet my school friend Helen and her boyfriend Ian at a tequila bar after. Later still we eat Thai. Tom shows me a photograph across the table of a grey horse under a tree. The horse is head down to the night, nibbling his foreleg. His tail is twisted maypole ribbons. His coat is the fabric of the play pony my mum stitched a long time ago. It had a stick neck and stick withers, stick shoulders and flank. It had my fetlocks and knees and the quiet hooves of two tennis shoes. Its grey face was bridled with gold rope. When you blew softly in its nostrils my play pony quivered. I saddled the horse with equestrian tales borrowed from the library I visited every Saturday morning. At home, when we jumped the rake-and-broom fences held high on the stiff backs of plastic garden chairs, we jumped straight out of those pages. Tom's photograph makes me lean forward like that. I talk to him about anything I can think of, fingers light around my nuzzling chopsticks.

Maybe it's the worry we'll outgrow the day that makes me collect and go back to the boat by myself. I deal all the rugs and pillows from the metal hold outside onto the floor of the children's corner and lock myself in. Perfectly still in my sleeping bag, I shine a torch to the ceiling until its sun shunts the night away and I can sleep. No 5 a.m. dive bombs. I wake long past that and it's time to move on.

28

PLAY (part i)

Out of London, leaving Limehouse and the floating quadrats that turn out to be rubbish traps on the grey road of the river, I can live in my head for days again. I go up and down its stairs and around all the rooms I'm busy decorating. I'm trying to curate all the things I've read and heard and seen on this trip, to arrange them in a way that will be helpful and pleasing to me. So I have essays by Montaigne carpeting entire wings, the pelt of a favourite Russian novel draped over a chair, lamps throwing shades of grey skies and bright ones and starry ones. I've shoved The Acquisitor into the cupboard under the stairs until I figure out where he goes. There's some handsome furniture that I've carved strangers' kindnesses into and lots of tureens filled with odd memories that I don't want to pour away just yet. Nothing exciting — just splashes of conversation, at a lock maybe, or the satisfying exhaustion that seems to puddle on the floor with my kicked-off clothes when I go to bed.

There's an interiors book on the boat that

I've never managed to sell, by Sibella Court. It's called *Nomad*. In it, she explains how travel mementos can be carefully exhibited back at home. I think this is what gives me the idea of consciously arranging little mental souvenirs into something splendid even if, unlike one of her show houses, no one will see inside my head but me. Court's isn't a new idea. It follows a tradition that started in Renaissance Europe of encyclopaedically collecting bones, relics, art, feathers, maps, stuffed dodos, precious stones, medical anomalies, *anything* that excited curiosity or awe or thought. The Germans called these Wunder-kammer ('wonder-rooms') in that precise way of theirs. They were microcosms of their owners' interests, experiences, dreams and profound fears. One of the reasons I fell in love with independent bookselling is that most shops are shelved in the same spirit.

Is there anything wrong with doing this in our heads too? I don't think so. Standing on the back of my boat, life imagined is as rich, if not more, than the one I'm grazing through on my way to the Kennet and Avon Canal. Another reason I love bookshops is because their owners must think this too. They must know the pulse of make-believe. Behind all those book spines they must see how the stories hold us tall. I'm with Dickens on the performative side of reading. A good book is mind theatre. Reading should be like a play.

⋆ ⋆ ⋆

A couple of days before leaving London I went to a London bookshop talk about narrow boating and real tennis delivered by certain members of the rock band Razorlight. It was useful for two reasons. First, I was out of diesel and had booked my passage up the Thames two days later. Panicked phone calls failed to produce any marine diesel dispensers in the area that would be open before then and I was glumly staring at the prospect of a five-litre jerry can and a twenty-minute walk to the nearest Shell garage — a trip I'd have to repeat at least six or seven times to get a decent level of fuel in the tank. By happy coincidence I was complaining of this injustice loudly to Stu, who had also come down for the talk, when the man sitting to our left beamingly introduced himself as a member of St Pancras Cruising Club, just two minutes up the canal from my current mooring. I had actually called the club earlier that day — only to be sternly told that just one member had permission to dispense diesel and he wouldn't be contactable until after the weekend. In fact, here he was. He opened up under cover of darkness the next night — and even stood a drink in the members' bar after. He was utterly charming.

The second of that evening's uncanny beneficences was the talk itself. Frontman Johnny Borrell et al had commandeered a narrow boat down a stretch of the Thames as part of a real tennis tour, stopping at the few courts the country still has along the way and presenting slides of their bizarre and booze-filled journey. Curiously, one of these courts was at Hardwick House, believed to be the inspiration for *The Wind in the Willows'* Toad Hall. Borrell talked briefly about the house, the history of real tennis and the confusing details of how actually you play the game. Mainly though, he talked about the concept of 'play' itself and I was surprised to hear how close his thoughts were to mine: play is fine, play is healthy, play is absolute licence to indulge in the pleasures of life.

I find it fitting that the book I sell more than any other on the boat is *The Wind in the Willows*. Kenneth Grahame's life was an odd one. He started writing the classic kids' tale of riverside adventure just a year after he was almost killed by a gunman who entered the Bank of England, where he worked as its secretary. Nowadays, the story is read as a paean to innocence and country pleasures. At

146

the time, probably still reeling from that altercation in the office, Grahame must have invested even more meaning in it — the book was a retreat from the terrors of the wider world.

In fact, Grahame's reluctance to interact with it, as adulthood demands, began much, much earlier. From his late teens he was already collecting what would amount to a flat-filling menagerie of toys and fluffy playthings. He started writing too — and his stories extolled the rural pleasures he'd enjoyed as a boy at his grandmother's Thames-side home, hitting out at modernity and machines as grave threats to a man's happiness and spiritual fulfilment.

Grahame shamelessly indulged his inner child. Even in his relationships. He married the bonkers daughter of the inventor of the pneumatic tyre when he was thirty-eight and still, by all accounts, a virgin. Elspeth was three years his junior but more than a match for him in nuttiness. They exchanged court-ship letters in a cringey child dialect and a crossfire of hideous nicknames. 'Darlin Minkie,' Grahame wrote one day, 'I ad nuther good nite & avnt ardly corfd torl terday — but it aint so nice a day & doesn't tempt one out.'

After the birth of their only son Alastair, Kenneth and Elspeth projected their infantile delusions upon him too. He was born blind in one eye, with a squint in the other, and grew up with massive behavioural problems including a penchant for lying in front of approaching traffic and for taking the name 'Robinson' — the same as his father's lunatic attacker. To his parents he was simply 'Mouse' — and a genius. Alastair killed himself at the age of nineteen while studying at Oxford University. His body was found, decapitated, on the railway line.

The Wind in the Willows was written for Alastair. As gifts from fathers go, it's almost unparalleled in its indulgence and remarkable potential for pleasure — even today. More than a century after it was published, Toad's unstable energy has proven to enjoy a curiously long half-life. We see our own nervousness to adapt through Mole's thick lenses. We identify with gruff, cudgel-wielding Badger's intolerance of other people. We Google 'narrow boats for sale' with Ratty's exuberant cry still ringing in our ears for truly, 'There is nothing, absolutely nothing, half so much worth doing as simply messing about in boats.'

Yes, as gifts from fathers go, *The Wind in the Willows* is up there with the best. 'Almost unparalleled,' I wrote. Almost. In fact, mine gave me a similarly good'un.

29

PLAY (part ii)

Having been politely, but consistently, turned down for bank loans to buy the boat, I can still remember my surprise when my parents offered to put up the capital instead. My father has always been cautious with money. He used to spend most of his Saturdays sweeping the local pound shop for toothbrushes with inflexible bristles and for batteries that were invariably outlived by the mayfly. I think I first started doubting the existence of Father Christmas when Diareze-branded stationery started appearing in my stocking from the free haul he'd receive from drug reps at work.

Yet both he and my mother have nonetheless always been generous people. They have a sixth sense for when their children's bank accounts are avalanching into overdraft and we find timely cash injections, which I'm often too ashamed to thank them for properly. A boat though — that's another league. We agreed a repayment strategy but after just six months of trading it became apparent that, to bastardise a popular saying, it's a gift that keeps on giving no return. Stu was also lavish with his finances. A scrupulous saver, he threw thirteen years of his hard-earned dollars at turning sixty feet of slowly rusting steel into a fully functional bookshop in just four months. And then there were the painting hours they all put in, the enormous paving slabs we hauled over precarious jetties for ballast, the floor-laying, fascia-building, soft furnishings sewing, two new staircases, partition walls to pull out, central heating and electrical work to be completed, an unwanted cassette toilet to clean up and store in a garage. A gas hob, sink, shower cubicle, cupboards and a four-foot-wide bed all also went. In their place, hundreds and hundreds of books given largely free of charge by complete strangers in response to a plea I placed in the local newspaper. People power, I learnt then for the first time, is some force.

But it's parents I want to return to here. When the bookshop opened, the enterprise had already begun to shape up as much more than a retail proposition. In the previous six months its idea had captured me in a way nothing else had since that hobby-horse equestrianism. It was a fantasy job, an indulgence, a constant daydream, a beautiful,

beautiful game. It is your parents who allow you to be a child. Mine were letting me keep hold of its best parts, even mid-twenties.

I tried reading *The Complete Guide to Starting and Running a Bookshop* to verse me in sales and potential market and running costs and other financial considerations but stopped soon after the second paragraph with an audible 'pshht'. The chapter title in itself — 'The business of bookselling' — I took as a personal threat to my carefully imagined idyll. Rereading it now, I realise a proper study would have saved me cash, confusion and no small amount of custom. It's sensible stuff. It even tells you right up front in figure 1.2 not to bother with the book trade if you don't have the following skills:

- Business skills: spotting profitable opportunities / negotiating good terms with suppliers
- Management skills: controlling and directing the business / planning and implementation
- Financial skills: running business accounts / controlling costs
- People skills . . .
- IT skills . . .
- Marketing skills . . .
- The list goes on.

It'll come as no surprise by now that I didn't — still don't — possess any of those. I concentrated instead on buying an old cash register and contemplating all the entrancing titles the boat would stock. Books, lots of — and somewhere to put the money. That should just about cover it. It was a naïve, infantile approach but, for that first summer at least, it worked. Sales surpassed our expectations. I cycled home each evening with takings rattling against the tin in the front wicker basket, chin back, the chain tick, tick, ticking in approval. It was *The Golden Age* — the title Kenneth Grahame took for one of his earlier books. The world was 'brimming' just as he described.

Chugging back up the Thames more than three years later I wonder if now is the right time to close shop. After the success of London it'd perhaps be fitting to stop now. My retail foray would at least be bookended with decent takings and happy memories. It's not yet August and the three months still looming on the trip seem suddenly appalling. I can understand how going south made sound business sense but bobbing across the West Country for weeks, then through Wales, Shropshire, spending a bit of time in Manchester, across the Pennines to Yorkshire and then all the way back down seems beyond me now. I sweep from elation to utter dejection. I board every window in my head. I think of nothing but the current I'm fighting to Reading. I pass out waiting for a lock in the rain. The lock keeper says, 'Take a rest here for a couple of hours,' but I just want to be off the river completely. He phones ahead to the next lock to keep an eye out for a black and cream narrow boat with a lawn on top.

I plan to stop in Windsor but a girl on Twitter has arranged for her boyfriend to meet me at Maidenhead to bring dinner. I give her my mobile number to pass on so he can suggest where I should moor and I continue. It takes much longer than I thought and turns dark. The whole time he sends messages that keep me going because they talk of chicken stir-fry, pudding, a Thermos flask of tea. I arrive gone 10 p.m. He cycles down to the river bank and rings his bell politely. He comes aboard with a basket of hot food that makes me want to sob.

Patch, his name is. He is maybe a couple of years younger than me and became a postman for the red bicycle before discovering the vehicles are being phased out. He has kept the cap but handed in his notice. He suggests phoning in sick the next day and hitching a ride up river to Henley with me and I couldn't be more pleased. Patch tells me about a birthday present he's making for his girlfriend. It's a wooden den frame, with each pole measurement scaled to her height. He'll put pink blankets over it in a park in London and they'll eat a picnic inside, faces flushed by its rosy glow. 'Why do people stop making dens as adults?' he asks. 'I don't know,' I say sadly, 'I haven't made one in years.' He laughs: 'But *this* is a den,' he says, 'this boat.'

30

PLAY (part iii)

What Patch says suddenly makes sense of everything. Dens don't just encourage imagination, they reinforce a sense of self. All that upturned furniture, the scrawled 'No adults' notices, they're a manifestation of who we are. I think of the rages I struggle to contain when people come aboard and continue conversations begun outside — about car repairs or their child's performance at school — instead of chameleoning to the quiet and the books. Or how I get irritated when visiting friends or family start rearranging stuff or plugging in phone chargers. I can hardly separate the boat from me now. I talk to it, as I talk to myself. Reflecting how hours earlier I was considering giving up, I grasp the impossibility.

There were so many dens in my childhood; the dusty floor under the purple bougainvillea bush, the sheeted, upturned sitting-room chairs, mezzanines in tree branches. Even away from home, my sister and I would find lairs. At the hospital pool we scaled a green pole to the changing-room roof and threw inflatables up to furnish our loft-style apartment. On the beach we pioneered the most sophisticated game of House known to pre-pubescence. Sandcastles were left behind: our property development had shifted from medieval to modern chic. We wanted Hockney pools and claimed them in the limpet-lived luxury of sea-trapping rocks. We squatted barnacled bedrooms, ensuite bathrooms, admiring each other's choices with all the solemnity of borrowed TV phrases: 'Triple aspect,' I would coo, pirouetting on a basalt chimney we had gleefully named a Period Feature. There were penthouses, palaces, a charming pied-à-terre. We sold seashells and unreal estate, dream homes by the sea.

There was even a boat den then. Wresting the ladder from the bunk bed we shared to circumnavigate the world would have been Rebecca's idea. She was a Midas of childhood entertainment: everything she touched turned to gaming gold. Laying it horizontally on the balding carpet tiles of our bedroom floor, we claimed a cabin each between the cheap pine rungs and cast off with milk teeth chatter and a half-empty bag of cornflakes. It was easy. In our imaginations we slipped away through the burglar guards on the window, over the

156

seabed of our red-tiled roller-boot route outside. There was the wave of a long driveway to curl us over the road. And then a blue diorama of sea and sky, me and her. We were barefooted, bathing-costumed adventurers together. We played Vasco da Gama. We got shipwrecked. We did scurvy knees and laughed ourselves off the raft.

When I see narrow boats I think of ladders. Of that ladder. Long and flat-bottomed, they share the same wrong shape for a water vehicle. They were built to work, to carry; coal, beer, tired feet to bed. When I saw Joseph, the boat that would become The Book Barge, I thought it could carry a dream. Dens are built like this. They're not houses — functional, clean, stable — they're places we inhabit for what they can *do*. They're transporting. They're places to get carried away in.

31

TERRORS

There are a total of 105 locks between Reading, where I rejoin the canal, and Bristol, which is where I'm slowly heading. Included in these is the famous Caen Hill flight, a twenty-nine-lock, five- to six-hour tribulation that I don't doubt I'll be carrying out drenched by rain. I am not wrong. These stats so distress me when I discover them in a guidebook outside Reading that I crash straight into a low-hanging tree and a branch wedges itself on the throttle, pushing the boat into full acceleration, nose to towpath. Forced face down onto the stern to avoid decapitation by another wooden limb, I hear the unmanned tiller bar slapped sideways by a third timber villain. We're caught in this standoff for a couple of minutes: the bookshop ramming the bank, the bank stonewalling its progress. A mother and small child watch on in horror. Hostage to hyperbole, I summon all my recollections of crap 90s movie sequel *Speed 2: Cruise Control* to wriggle out of potential dismemberment, vehicular carnage and certain embarrassment because this is ALMOST EXACTLY THE SAME SCENARIO as Jason Patric helming a cruise ship askance of an oil tanker and into the Caribbean island of Saint Martin on a $110 million stunt budget. What did Sandra Bullock do? Regret starring in this? Receive a Razzie? Grab a chainsaw! I crawl inside for the paper/hair scissors and hack at the gear-box branch with one of its blunt blades. Obviously, this chews through nothing more than my own ring finger so I employ Patric's technique of bow thrusters to turn the boat, and my own barge pole ingenuity to lever the branch away, and that's how The Book Barge makes an ignominious escape from Berkshire's county town. I plaster my hand and comb out the foliage and continue to Newbury.

Some miles before Hungerford a chainsaw actually does show up. I'm at a lock and two British Waterways guys are strimming the trees around a clearing, in which two figures are asleep in the centre. Between the noise of the cutters and the lock filling and my engine and the yelled conversation I'm having with the BW men, I don't know how the couple on the grass carry on snoozing, so I hang around after the lock until the men have finished and then tiptoe back to check they're actually alive. They are, and they're sitting up by this point eating something they describe as a nut burger, which is loose peanuts in a white, unbuttered bap. The couple — a boy and a girl in their early twenties — are walking from London to Stonehenge. They live in a self-built commune just outside the capital and the girl, mixed race and weighed down by an enormous rucksack, I think is the most beautiful person I've ever seen. They hitch a lift with me.

On the way we share stories about moneyless living, at which they're far more experienced than I. The girl tells me about a woman called Peace Pilgrim who inspired her own decision to live differently from others. Peace Pilgrim, born Mildred Lisette Norman, was an American brought up on a poultry farm in New Jersey. On 1st January 1953, with the Korean War having just kicked off, she set out on what would become a twenty-eight-year walk back and forth across the United States — for peace. She carried no money, no food and just the limited possessions she could fit in the pockets of her blue Peace Pilgrim tunic. In order for the world to become peaceful, she said, *people* must become more peaceful. This seems pretty obvious. But, she added, 'It always comes back to the thing so many of us wish to avoid: working to improve ourselves.' Ironically, having spent so much of her life on foot, Peace Pilgrim died in a car crash. She was being driven to a speaking engagement in Indiana.

The girl asks if I'm narrow boating the UK for peace. 'No,' I have to admit. 'Then you're working to improve yourself,' she says. I want to kiss her. I drop them off at Hungerford. She carries on to Stonehenge but the boy has to head home to pet-sit his mum's cat, which makes me laugh a little cruelly.

I moor at Great Bedwyn that night and have the most terrifying nightmare that has nothing at all to do with peace. In it, a serial killer has got off the train at the village station and walked across to my mooring by the skips for boaters' rubbish. He stands on the towpath looking at my boat for a long time. In one hand he holds a semi-automatic pistol, and in the other a hunting rifle. It's this second one he uses to blast the porthole window above my head into a thousand blood diamonds. He does this to the rectangular window to its right, and to the one next to that, and the one next to that at the far end of the boat, just above the shelf of poetry. All the four windows on that side of the boat are now blown out. I jerk out of my sleeping bag and smash a window on the other side, the one above the kids' area, and tumble into the water. When I try swimming away the man sends bullets into the water to catch my legs. I put my whole head under and feel my way back along the boat to roughly its middle. Here I stop and surface and hold onto the gunwales while my assailant's thin smile keeps shooting fear into me.

Even after waking from this dream I can't shake the horror of him being outside still. I grab my phone from under the pillow and ball down at the toe of my sleeping bag with it. I hold it in my hand for ten minutes, trying to hear the man with his guns by the bins, too scared to call anyone. I have Stu's number up ready and, when I do call him, I whisper the bloodbath that took place in case the killer hears me. Stu's voice is small and tired on the other end but it is enough. When I hang up I can flick on a torch and cry.

32

HERON

Another day I'm waiting for a lock to fill up and start talking to a heron, who's skulking by some reeds just below the far gate. Something not many people know about herons is that they are also known as shitepokes because they defecate when frightened from their cover. Something still fewer people know is that an old English word for them is hernshaw, which is very similar to my surname. With our shared cowardice and etymology and canalside habitats, I feel a certain kinship with these birds, who are rapidly becoming my second favourite after pigeons.

The heron, who doesn't like being disturbed, says I can ask him just three questions. I hate being put on the spot like this. I can't think of anything. 'Would you rather be a pigeon or . . . ' I begin, but I can't think of another bird off the top of the head so I leave it like that. My next question is whether he knows who Christopher Walken, the actor, is. Finally I ask him if he's ever killed a man. He answers negative to all three and I think I know him a bit better.

'Now ask me three questions,' I say. So he asks where I've come from today and where I'm hoping to moor tonight and how long my boat is, which is pretty much all anyone asks on the canal. Just as I'm telling him, a guy with a long cream coat steps out from over the top of the bridge. He looks around and then shouts, 'Are you on your own, young lady?' Even though I've just been talking aloud and he probably heard, I can't get the lie out on time. So I just mumble, 'Yes.' And then he smirks and walks down the bridge and towards me. When he's right in front of me he looks around furtively again and then says, 'I've got something under my coat that may interest you.' I'm tempted to scream or run away at this point but I don't want to scare the heron, who may shit himself, and am desperate to prove my courage for the both of us. So I tense all my muscles to punch him with instead if he makes one false or rape-suggestive move.

As I feared he starts slowly unbuttoning his coat but all that's under there is a windlass holster, which he pelvic thrusts with a loud 'ta-da!' I'm annoyed he gave me such a scare and interrupted my chat with the heron, who now flies off. But he seems chatty enough himself so I tell him where I've come from and where I'm going to and that my boat's sixty foot long. I want to ask him if he thinks all herons look a bit like Christopher Walken too but I get shy and just jump back on the boat after he's helped with the lock and wave and say thanks and wish him a nice day.

33

WWJD?

It is a truth universally acknowledged, that a single man in possession of a good fortune, must be in want of a wife. It is a view less commonly asserted that a single woman in possession of a good-sized narrow boat must be in want of a husband. On the way to Bath I receive this wisdom from a stranger. She and her husband are travelling back up the canal from Bristol when we meet as I'm halfway through a lock. While her husband holds back with their boat, the woman walks towards mine and starts winding up the paddles on her side, for which I thank her profusely. I do the same on my side and then, as is customary, sit on the gate staring despondently at the emptying torrent. This is when the woman heads over the bridge to my side, ostensibly to pass the time chatting. In fact, it is to reprimand me in the most severe terms for my 'selfishness' in driving a narrow boat single-handed.

'Have you not got a boyfriend or husband?' she storms.

'Nope, just me I'm afraid.'

'Then have you no idea how narcissistic you're being?'

'For my lack of life partner??' I'm not following her reasoning.

'For holding up every other boater on this canal by insisting upon doing it yourself. Don't you know that it takes a single-handed boater at least twice as long operating a lock as anyone else?'

'I'm afraid needs must. It's hardly selfish taking on extra work for myself is it?'

'But you single people don't!' She is raging good and proper by now.

'Eh?'

'Who was it who winded the paddles up for you just now? ME! And who'll be opening half the gate for you in two minutes? ME! It's extra work *for innocent cruisers* — not for you. I don't mind so much when a *man* is canalling alone but girls. They're just hassle for the whole system. You're young — can't you just get yourself a man and do us all a favour?'

★   ★   ★

Lucky for this woman I have spent the last few days of this trip, which will take me to Bath in the next day or so, in conscientious study of the writings of its former resident Jane Austen. It has struck me recently that my inland waterwayfaring has perhaps fostered a little in the way of uncouthness about my character, which normally gusts from shy to recessive but is largely of sound please/thank you foundations. Just yesterday I surprised both Joseph and myself by commanding a grumpy fisherman to 'Piss off, asshole' when he lashed the side of the boat with his rod for allegedly going too fast. Later, I urinated in a trough of pansies behind a teashop (closed, or I would naturally have snuck in and commandeered a rest room). Slightly ashamed of both, I've vowed to nurture a spirit of forbearance and propriety, at least until I've left Bath behind. To this end, I've inked the letters W, W, J and D to the knuckles of both hands: What Would Jane Do?

Despite our tendency to view her novels as happy-ever-after love stories, Jane Austen was not a romantic. She was a realist. Although she rejected a financially suitable match in 1802 because she professed not to love the man, she never pursued relations with a suitor she *did* have feelings for, Tom Lefroy, because he was dependent on a great-uncle for funds. Jane would probably concede that the lady at the lock had a point: a bit of brawn would make my current life a lot easier. However, she also preached delicacy to the feelings of other people, which could justify my fist leaving a faint retaliatory smudge of WWJD in the woman's jaw for her insulting behaviour. But I have different plans.

When the lock empties I open my side of the gate, whistle my way down the ladder and slip inside for two minutes to change into a shorter skirt, apply a lick of mascara and gloss my lips a shade redder. Steering out I give the woman a cheery wave before sidling up to her husband's boat and flicking mine into reverse until I'm perfectly level with him at his tiller. 'Hello', I coo, 'I hope you don't mind me stopping like this but your boat's so awfully big and handsome that I couldn't carry on without complimenting you. You must be *very* strong to steer this all by yourself. And so clever to lift your fenders up whereas all mine have snapped off. And would you mind *very much* showing me what wax you apply to keep the paintwork so shiny?' So we chat like this for five or so minutes, my tinkling laughter just loud enough to carry to the far gate of the lock, where his wife seethes and stares. Then I grab his wrist, feign surprise at the time on his watch, and push into acceleration with a departing: 'You must thank your lovely wife for being so *patient!* I've kept you here far too long and she was so very *kind* to me back there. Please pass on my thanks.' I blow a kiss.

However, the woman's words have given pause for thought and I consider the convenience of getting a guy aboard to work the canal while I sit back surveying the moral landscape of *Sense and Sensibility*. I act fast, not forgetting Austen once described Elizabeth Elliot in *Persuasion*, still single at twenty-nine, as approaching 'the years of danger'. At twenty-eight I am already a year older than Charlotte Lucas in *Pride and Prejudice*, who settles for boorish Mr Collins for fear *her* time is running out. When a lone kayaker comes into view I look with tenderness and delight on his beautiful and smiling, albeit sweaty, countenance and interesting manner and invite him on *tout de suite*. I am not yet four-and-twenty, I lie to lure him, and flutter my lashes wildly in an effort to manufacture some Bennet-esque 'fine eyes' bewitchment. He gallantly salutes, heaving his boat onto my roof and grabbing my proffered windlass at the next flight of locks. I imagine evoking this scene to family and friends when I introduce him as my new boyfriend. 'And when, exactly, did you fall in love with him,' they'd ask. 'It has been coming on so gradually, that I hardly know when it began,' I'd say coyly. 'But I believe I must date it from my first seeing his beautiful biceps working the five locks at Seend.'

Unfortunately, the relationship quickly sours when he suggests continuing the journey with me all the way to Bradford on Avon. Too polite to refuse, I endure until Hilperton Marina where I send him out to get sweets and fizzy pop, unload his kayak with the help of a passer-by and, on seeing him return, shout out that I've been called away on urgent book-selling business and cast off quite alone and overwhelmingly relieved. I continue in this happy solitude for the rest of the day, reading aloud to Joseph from the start of *Emma* and recalling what Rudyard Kipling once wrote of Austen's soothing quality: 'There's no one to match Jane when you're in a tight place.'

I think of these words when I finally make Bath and moor on the Avon next to the rugby club, in the shadow of Pulteney Bridge. Since leaving London I've been travelling more days than been open as a bookshop. What funds I accumulated down south are gone and the bank rings hourly to chase charges and unpaid loans. When Laura visits she's optimistic the city's literary heritage will soon serve up success, so I pay for a week's mooring and sneak a shower in the nearby leisure centre. Then we link arms and look in shop windows until, through one, I see something more becoming of a Janeite than my leggings and oil-stained T-shirt. Having consulted the knuckle oracle one last time, I spend my remaining £30 on a new frock with absolute peace of mind.

WWJD? Declaim its length but adore the pretty blue-and-pink print.

34

MONEY

Bath is as good as Laura's word. That there is a waist-height metal safety rail to scale on this riverbank before clambering aboard doesn't deter custom. Even the mayor, the Right Worshipful Bryan, pays a visit, hailing Joseph 'Queen of the River' — although not in the slighting way in which it is interpreted by Joseph. Joseph is furious. Nothing I can say about his gender anomaly in the world of boating makes it right. Joseph wants revenge and, confirming long-held suspicions about his Goth sympathies (the black costume, the antipathy for chat), he wants to wreak it in a weird, dark — and surprisingly Bath-specific — way: by making a curse tablet.

Typically, curse tablets were messages scratched into metal requesting intervention from the gods to right wrongs and punish crimes. They were often written in code or backwards or with lines pointing in alternating directions. Archaeologists have recovered several examples from the site of the Roman Baths' main spring, which was once a shrine to the goddess Sulis. Another, recovered from the Temple at Bath, reads: 'Dodimedis has lost two gloves. He asks that the person who has stolen them should lose his mind and eyes in the temple where she appoint.' Contextually then, the opprobrium Joseph heaps on the mayor makes more sense. Innocuous as his comment was, if it's okay to damn a person to mental disarray and physical blindness for picking up the wrong pair of gloves, I guess we can make Bryan suffer for the ambiguity of his praise. So Joseph dictates, and I scratch below his waterline:

Mayor Bryan called Joseph a girl. He's not. He asks that Bryan be knotted in the chains of his office and thrown to the river.

Except that I forget to write it backwards so have to make a second attempt on the other side:

royaM nayrB dellac hpesoJ a lrig. s'eH ton. eH sksa taht nayrB eb dettonk ni eht sniahc fo sih eciffo dna nworht ot eht revir.

Both content that justice has been served, I go back to selling books and rejecting bank calls while Joseph continues reading *The Sandman*.

During my time in Bath I reflect on Ezra Pound's assertion that, in our time, 'the curse is monetary illiteracy, just as inability to read

174

plain print was the curse of earlier centuries'. I wonder if he's right. Not everyone, of course, is afflicted. My old school friend and her partner — both accountants — pay a visit and spend a lot of the time on their phones asking for mortgage quotes for the house they're buying — a beautiful, jaw-droppingly priced one-bed North London flat. This would suggest some of us can read finances just fine. But elsewhere there are signs that I'm not alone in penury. While I'm in Bath violent riots in London are copycatted across the country — even in Bristol, where I'm headed next. Shops are looted of mobile phones and expensive trainers and enormous flat-screen TVs to be taken home or resold on the black market after the empty shelves are set alight to stoke front pages of newspapers and the rolling headlines of twenty-four-hour television coverage. The weird thing is that no one seems entirely sure what's caused the unrest. Heavy-handed policing? Gang culture? Economic stagnation? Youth unemployment? Perhaps the only clear picture is acute frustration with the way things are turning out for people of my generation who are finally united, it seems, in being broke, Blackberry-glued and bent on somehow changing the whole crappy system we live with. And I can't help but be quietly thrilled.

We were born in the boom time for capitalism and greed. We grew up watching films that were obsessed with money, from *Wall Street* to *Pretty Woman* to pretty much any film starring Tom Cruise, which always seemed somehow to espouse the rewards of cocky entrepreneurialism. Except in *Top Gun*, where he was just cocky. And so when we worked hard at school and went to college or university and tried it out in the workplace and got nowhere, we thought, eh? And so we tried harder. We tried our own businesses. I tried bookselling and, though I was never dumb enough to go into it for the millionaire-making potential, I did at least expect it to pay enough to survive. And I was wrong. And that's when I gave up on money altogether and started living by the book, which is a currency that suits me much better.

However, it hasn't solved the backlog of debt I've brought with me. Even though I'm surviving quite nicely by swapping stock for pizza and Pinot, and only occasionally feel the need to loot the till for traditional tender for a new dress, I'm still being threatened with court action, harassed by telephone and, in the eyes of most of society, am just a bum on a boat who isn't paying taxes. And that annoys me. I suspect the rioters feel much the same.

176

As well as curse tablets, people used to throw money in Bath's Sacred Spring as offerings to the goddess. More than 12,000 Roman coins, the largest votive deposit known in Britain, have been found. What's the difference, I'm wondering, as my phone starts screaming again when I'm out for a quick walk near Pulteney Bridge. I pull it from the bottom of my handbag, along with a couple of pennies. The bottom of my handbag is where most pennies seem to go to die. I throw them into the weir below and their splash is lost in the tussle of spray. I once read a beautiful sentence that described how sunlight 'coins' on the water, which I always think of when the light and the water's just right, like now. I turn my phone off and feel the curse lifting. Just slightly. Or maybe it's because my bag's now two pence less heavy on my shoulder. Whatever, it's a nice feeling.

35

BRISTOL

In terms of delivering new financial systems, Bristol seems the place to be. Chugging there from Bath, which takes an entire day, I read up about the Bristol Pound scheme they're asking local businesses to sign up to. It's to be a complementary currency for the city aimed specifically at boosting the local economy and is backed pound for pound by sterling deposits, so carries no more financial risk than most banking institutions. Since visiting with The Book Barge in August 2011, the currency has officially launched and, to date, has over £B140,000 circulating around Bristol, with Electronic Bristol Pounds (payments made by text and online transfer) accounting for over half of that figure. Even the mayor has his salary paid in it. As well as supporting local traders (chain stores can't take part), its founders argue the voluntary tender also carries environmental benefits by reducing the amount of goods that require transportation up and down the country.

There are other reasons I'm already a little

in love with Bristol. It's the closest Joseph will ever have come to the coast. We'll be moored alongside seafaring boats, including the SS *Great Britain*. There'll be seagulls clouding the tops of buildings and flash mobbing the crust of a tuna sandwich on the pavements. And then there's a family connection — my dad was brought up here. And a literary one — *Treasure Island*, a favourite childhood book, was partly set here. Harvey's Bristol Cream will bubble from public fountains and the spirit of John Cabot, explorer extraordinaire, will scent the air with adventure. What's more, it's home to one of the most delightfully named bookshops I've ever chanced upon — Bloom & Curll, on 74 Colston Street. As well as its eclectic stock, it promises free space to 'display fine art, discuss politics, poetry, Kafka or have a cup of tea, play chess and plan the next revolution'. I squeeze the tiller bar harder and anticipate the greatest things.

With its own port authority, Bristol doesn't come under the jurisdiction of British Waterways, to whom I pay my trading licence. As such, on entering the city I have to fork out and fill in some separate paperwork to give me a week's mooring. The lock keeper is enthusiastic about the idea of a floating bookshop and suggests settling by the

Arnolfini arts centre, where I should capture a lot of custom. He also gives details about exiting the city another way — up the Bristol Channel — rather than crawling back along the canal I've just come down and which the muscle in my right, lock-paddle-winching shoulder still protests painfully against. I tie up as suggested and head off to meet some girls who visited the boat in Bath. 'FREE CANAPÉS!!!' they have excitedly promised in a text message from a gallery opening. Bristol, I love you. Closing up, all the sun-bared legs overhanging the quayside, drinks held lightly over a hundred knees, seem like just another row of exclamations.

My first priority on opening shop the next morning is to get hold of a ticket to the Bristol Old Vic's production of *Treasure Island*. It's to be an outdoor show because of refurbishment work inside the theatre build-ing, and probably the better for it. I think of the epitaph on Robert Louis Stevenson's Samoan grave taken from his own poem *Requiem*, which celebrates resting 'Under the wide and starry sky'. What better curtains to end the show than darkness falling quietly on King Street. My obsession with Stevenson is one of my longest literary affairs. I read *Treasure Island* as a little girl, starting it on a sick day from school. I had earache and so one side of my head was pressed into a hot-water bottle on my pillow while a hand held the library book open over the edge of the bed. It was an awkward position to start an adventure but Stevenson didn't seem to mind how I came to it. He just galloped on through the story, throwing parrots at me and one-legged pirates, buccaneers and buried gold and drunken seamen called Billy Bones who dropped dead. I loved it all — the breathless plot and peculiar language, and especially Ben Gunn's strange plea for cheddar: 'You mightn't happen to have a piece of cheese about you, now?' I read *Kidnapped* after that, then *Jekyll and Hyde*. As I got older, I started reading about Stevenson's life too, and finding out that his compulsive story-writing was born from an early life consigned to bed with coughs and fevers, I remembered my own unhealthy discovery all those years ago. I have a torn newspaper write-up of Stevenson's life hanging on my wall at home. It's by the crime writer Ian Rankin, who idolises him too. Rankin said our hero used both travel and the imagination as 'a prophylactic against pain', which seems the best kind of medicine.

Stevenson's first published work was called *An Inland Voyage*. It was an account of a journey he made by canoe from Antwerp to

Northern France, where he ended up meeting his cougar wife Fanny, a married American with two kids who was eleven years his senior. When I set out from Staffordshire in May, Stevenson's trip gave me confidence that wandering the canals of a country can be a prelude to a life of more exotic travel and opportunity. When I got home, I tried buying a Shetland pony, whom I envisaged as a latter-day Modestine to recreate *Travels with a Donkey in the Cevennes*. The owner refused to sell her to me when I admitted I had no place but a narrow boat to stable her. Years of American and Pacific travel followed the French trips for Stevenson and his new family, before they eventually settled in Samoa. He died following a struggle to open a bottle of wine — a passing only bettered by Dylan Thomas's topping by eighteen straight whiskies.

I procure tickets to *Treasure Island* with an ease that makes me wonder if the pirate gods themselves hadn't black magic'ed it: a couple walk aboard wearing T-shirts advertising the show. When questioned, they reveal they're ushers at the theatre. They leave with the largest haul of books I've ever gifted and I sit back with a ticket for tomorrow's show in my hand. In the end, I go twice. I enjoy it so much the first time I insist Laura drives over to see it again the next night. It whips up a restlessness. It makes me uncharacteristically bold. It sets my course of action as sure as the *Hispaniola's* for the strange events that follow in this most swashbuckling of cities.

36

FRIENDS

I'm banned from trading in Bristol. That's what the harbour master tells me. He says the lock keeper I paid my licence to should never have given the impression that selling books from a boat would be okay. It's not. 'But — .'

'No. Just no.' I can stay in the harbour and enjoy a holiday or I can leave. Except I can't do the latter because British Waterways have closed off a lock before Bath for the next week to carry out maintenance and my passage up the Channel is only booked for five days hence. I'm trapped, untrading, precisely where I am. Bollocks.

I take a deckchair out onto the bow of the boat and sit with my feet up, the skin under my ankles getting slowly scorched because the black of the boat's paint stores heat like an apocalypse prepper. I try to feel like I'm on holiday. A busker playing saxophone on the bridge opposite is hailing the morning with a rendition of Paul McCartney's *Yesterday*, which is not wholly unpleasant. When he moves on to *Somewhere Over the*

Rainbow, that's a little harder to take. I go inside, fetch a book, and try again. I'm on holiday. I'm on holiday. I'm on holiday. In my peripheral vision I can make out some consternation on the quayside. People are crowding and pointing to something in the river and, at one point, an orange life ring is thrown in, but that doesn't concern me. I'm on holiday. The sky is the blue of a cosmetic-counter nail polish. It looks too even, too bright, too *teenage*. A couple of cotton-wool clouds are brushing over it but even their acetone scrub isn't removing anything. This is what holidays look like, I tell myself. It's been nearly three years since I had one because of the shop, so forgive my difficulty recognising it.

'Oi! OOOOIIIIIII! YOU! On the boat! Don't just sit there! DO SOMETHING!' I look up quickly.

'Me? Are you talking to me?'

I look around but there's no one else the hatred of fifty-plus pairs of narrowed eyes on the bank seems directed towards. Now they have my attention they're all talking at once and I feel trapped between the wall of their histrionics and the slow murdering of Judy Garland over on the bridge.

'What do you want?' I holler back. I'm on holiday for *one day*. 'WHAT DO YOU

WANT?!' I follow the line of their stabbing fingers and pick out the life ring in the water and, next to it, something winged and wet and obviously drowning. I step off the boat onto the pontoon for a closer look. I crouch down and squint my eyes. I am disbelieving. Is that — . . .

'Is that — . . . Is that a *pigeon?*'

They whoop on the quayside and jump up and down a bit. Yesitis, Yesitis, Yesitis, they squawk. And now I'm furious. 'I'M ON HOLIDAY!' I storm. 'AND YOU HONESTLY EXPECT ME TO RESCUE *ANOTHER* ONE?' But there's a hippyish-looking girl who's leading the mob and she's just as mad back.

'He's a *living creature*,' she screeches. 'He's *dying out there.*' So I huff and grab my barge pole, lie down on the pontoon, hook my feet over the far edge, wriggle my chest out over the water and field the pigeon into my empty hand with a deft thwack of the pole. When I hold him aloft the crowd goes wild. I keep the posture, head bowed, pigeon fist raised like a Black Power salute until even the saxophonist stops and begins a slow, admiring clap. Just a normal day's work, I want to tell them. And I realise, sadly, that the holiday must be over.

Once the pigeon is dispatched to a cardboard box to dry out on the roof of the boat, I turn on my laptop and begin a blog. *Book buyers of fair Bristol, it begins, your harbour master has refused permission to flog my literary wares to you. River trading is prohibited by ancient by-law, I have had explained. But I say: pssshhht. Come as friends, not customers, my dear, pigeon-loving brethren. Peruse my shelves and drink my tea and p-p-p-pick up a paperback and, if the mood takes you, leave a little friendly donation by the biscuit tin on your way out. What's £7.99 between 'friends'? Or buy me dinner. Or show me the sights. Or beer me to busting in your best bars. Let's be 'friends'. Text FRIEND to 079 . . . . . .*

When I've published it I go and hang out with the wino and his dog at the end of the pontoon. I tell him about the harbour master and he pontificates on the thickheadedness of Bristol port authorities. He swears he'll get revenge for me and I put my arm round his pet, who wears a jaunty kerchief for a collar, and feel much better about the city again. We raise plastic cups of warm Sauvignon and toast: 'To the most miserable bastard in the whole of Bristol.' But before I can drink it my phone beeps, and again, and twice more. And it keeps doing that all day. It seems The Book Barge has a whole heap of pals out there. I set appointment times and they come punctually

187

all afternoon, browsing the bookcases, offering vague veterinary advice about my tanning avian atop, choosing a couple of reads each and leaving a growing pile of gold pieces by the door. That evening I sift through all the offers of entertainment and accommodation in my inbox before settling on a home-cooked spaghetti Bolognese, DVD and early night in Clifton. Before my lift arrives I bring the pigeon into the boat, lay out a sprinkling of Alpen breakfast cereal and a tub of water by his unmoved head in a box, puncture the cardboard with air holes and Sellotape the top shut. Knowing he'll not last the night I can't at first bring myself to write his name on the side. But I do, fool. *Here lies Nelson III. Third time unlucky.*

37

CREW

Joseph lets me know something's wrong as soon as I see him from the top of the pontoon steps the next morning. He has this look about him, different from his usual scowl. He looks *traumatised*. There are rusty tear tracks down his cheeks. He leans ever so slightly to starboard as a tired runner nursing a stitch. When I unlock the bow doors I can see why. He's possessed! There's a *thing* in there flying off the walls, a kind of spirit creature. And a terrible smell of Tipp-Ex and cold roast dinner and gangrenous wound. I let out a squeal that's a bit muted by my fingers springing to peg both nostrils, and jump back onto the pontoon where I cling to Joseph's ropes, quivering with fear. The next minute, the demon itself flies out and I can see the cunning goblin has assumed the shape of a bird. I want to say something Latinate that sounds like an exorcism, but you don't pick up these kind of language skills in comprehensive schools any more so I make do with a courageous *Carpe Diem!*, which I first heard from Robin Williams banging on from the front of a classroom in *Dead Poets Society*. I repeat it three or four times so it sounds more like an incantation and less self-help. Either way, the incubus gets the idea and flutters off.

It's only when I head inside that I realise, rather than inadvertently mooring over a hell hole, Nelson III's only gone and resurrected! He's pumped a claw through the roof of the box and squeezed out to besmear the walls of the good ship with feather and Alpen and doo. The shelves have also taken a beating, with the one housing authors L — P suffering rather more than the others. The works of Iris Murdoch have to be removed from circulation immediately. I try to salvage the rest with a damp sponge and a spray of passionflower and black orchid Soft & Gentle antiperspirant, which seems to do the job. And all the time I'm thinking, hurrah! He lives! He flies another day! I'm dancing around the boat making strange laughing/yelping noises and I even take a running jump onto my black desk chair, which skates across to the new releases on its three little dusty black wheels — and tips, smacking my head against the corpulent body of David Foster Wallace's *The Pale King*.

These larks don't last. As I'm tackling some of the more stubborn stains with a multipack of Nivea face wipes, my friend with the dog shows up bearing bad news and a vandalised 'Crew Only' sign. While I was away yesterday evening the harbour fascists came by again with the new pontoon ruling, he relates, and to tell me to stop inviting 'friends' aboard on health and safety grounds. 'The bastards!' I cry. 'The dickbrains!' he echoes, and he proudly holds out the trophy of his midnight sabotage mission, which was hung, he explains, across the top of the pontoon steps. On his way out he lobs it overboard. It makes a satisfying plop in the water in the centre of the channel but I watch, horrified, as the current swings it incriminatingly back, where it floats all morning periodically sounding my hull like a gavel.

I take to the blog again as soon as the shop's cleared up. *Readers — nay, ALL RESIDENTS — of Bristol, jewel of the Avon, I plea. I've tried being friends . . . But it's just NOT ENOUGH. 'Crew' is what's wanted now: coxswains and bowhooks, petty officers and midshipmen, galley slaves, seamen, warrant officers and commodores. YOUR ADMIRAL NEEDS YOU! Scrub the decks, batten down the hatches, hoist the mizzen, splice the mainbrace and shiver me timbers. I don't care what pretext you adopt to come aboard but make sure you tell the son of a Biscuit Eater at the gates that you're only here to heave ho with all hands on deck and not to buy the books. Understood? At ease sailors.*

Well maybe I also added something about the harbour master being a bilge-sucking yo ho ho and that's what sent him over the edge because half an hour later there's a stern rapping on the hatch and two of Avon and Somerset Constabulary's finest in my shop. They're extremely tall and have to hunch slightly under the ceiling while they read out the section of archaic regulation that prevents a girl from selling under sail and explain how it's infinitely more hazardous to climb aboard a boat to buy Dr Seuss than pop pills and swig vodka on the 1959 German-built cargo ship-cum-nightclub Thekla, which is another working vessel moored just down river from me. I feel full of righteous indignation, as little Jim Hawkins must have felt listening to the outlines of Long John Silver's mutiny from inside the apple barrel. But I assume a mask of humility and promise to take down the 'inflammatory' material on my website and say thanks very much when one of the coppers compliments me on the retail outfit being 'much more professional than expected'. And when they're gone I scroll through my address book for the most powerful person I know, which in this case isn't Uri Geller, spoon bender and kindly interviewee in a past job, but the excellent Mayor Bryan of Bath, of course, who unwittingly left his business card in my hand last week. I don't breathe a whisper of this to Joseph. Still reeling from the pigeon haunting, I fear he would probably keelhaul me for this small treason.

And that's how, overnight, The Book Barge becomes 'The Boat that Bristol Banned' or, in a less pithily titled piece: 'The Floating Bookshop that Accepts Payment in Milk that Bristol Banned.' It makes not just waterways news but local media and the BBC website too. Laura calls excitedly from Cannock to tell me I've reached the heady heights of Ceefax, which no previous nor subsequent accomplishments will come close to beating. In truth, I actually feel a little embarrassed about the whole thing. And clearly Bristol City Council do too because they offer me a stall at their market for the rest of my stay — a very kind gesture that I accept with relief. The next day's breakfast headlines read: Bookshop v. Bristol — Truce Reached. We all trot off to work a little happier.

38

EXEUNT

In the end, leaving Bristol is a lot harder than I imagine. I can't say I especially enjoy hauling books to and from the harbour to my table at the Nails Market, but I do love being here and all the generous people who offer transport and tours of their city and stand drinks in its pubs and cook meals in their homes and still keep in touch today. I doubt the shop will receive a warmer welcome on its trip and I'm not proved wrong. On a more practical level, however, leaving Bristol is difficult because I can't actually afford to. Heading to Avonmouth and then up the Severn Estuary to Sharpness requires two pilots to navigate its strong currents and shifting sandbars. And pilots — usually ex-Merchant Navy types — don't come cheap. The ones I've hired are charging £300 for the trip. While my time in Bristol has been successful in terms of swaps (I've probably eaten, slept, drank and socialised better here than in any other port of call to date) it hasn't produced enough coffers to cover the cruise out.

And there's more. Calling to arrange where we should meet, the second pilot stresses I must be able to cover off all the elements on his safety checklist first. These include being equipped with the relevant charts, purging the fuel tank before filling up, replacing the oil filter, proof of an operational bilge pump, sealing the windows, vents and doors to ensure they're watertight, working navigation lights, hand flares, a hand bailer, long mooring lines, an anchor with chain and warp, marine band VHF and a full complement of fenders. When he finishes I stay very quiet. I hear him exhale, irritated, on the other end. 'If you're struggling, I can bring the charts and VHF,' he says. It's a start. I hang up and immediately ring Stu, in tears.

It's a testament to Stu's character — and the fact he knows me better than anyone after the nine years we were together — that his first words on seeing me cross-legged on the bow of the boat and knotting together balled pairs of my knee-length socks is not to laugh out loud. Instead he sits down beside me and wearily explains that even the best quality Aran yarn (only the finest hosiery on this ship, reader) offers no protection against the steel of another boat or the concrete of a lock wall smashing the side of Joseph. Hockey socks do not a sound fender make, he concludes. So I put them away. And I bring out a length of rope instead. We take an end each and knot in silence for at least an hour until something only slightly more convincing takes shape. This will do for one. Stu has the bright idea of recycling the two empty plastic milk cartons in the bin so we fill them up with water, noose the handles and now we're halfway there with three. Conjuring up another trio eludes us. I suggest all sorts of things, from the collected works of DH Lawrence in a plastic shopping bag to four months of cereal bars in a pillow case. In the end we simply gamble on putting all our current fenders on one side — the side the pilot will see when he jumps aboard. We figure he's unlikely to notice the far side is unprotected until we're under way. Fenders are crossed off the list. As are anchor (borrowed), hand flares (I have tea lights, matches, an air mattress pump and a Blue Peter make-do mentality) and bailer (plant pot with holes plugged by chewing gum). We can't see the logic of stressing too much over navigation lights as we'll be making the trip by daylight. As for long mooring lines, the only decent length we have has since shapeshifted into one of the fenders. If required, we'll just have to drop anchor for forty minutes while we unknot it.

As we're not quite sure what purging the fuel tank entails, Stu lends me money to just fill it up. He also covers the pilot costs. We buy a new oil filter and try to wrench the current one off, but only succeed in denting it. For the next twenty-four hours we take turns holding vigil in front of it, terrified we've punctured the metal casing and that the engine will fail halfway up the channel. We duct tape the windows, forward hatch, doors and vents, but it's crappy cheap stuff and most has billowed off before reaching Portishead Marina, where we wait for the tide and better sea conditions overnight — and where the second pilot will take over.

If The Book Barge, with its plastic-grassed roof and cargo of classic literature, looks out of place on the canals, you can only imagine its self-consciousness in a coastal marina of traditional fishing boats and super-expensive leisure yachts. Mooring tentatively, we feel the eyes of a dozen Dubarry-polo-shirted senior management types look up from a fresh coat of deck varnish towards our dangling milk bottles with quiet disgust. 'I didn't know they let narrow boats in here,' one man begins conversationally once we've tied up. 'In fact, I didn't know they let narrow boats out on open water.'

'It's a *book barge*,' I glower, as if that

197

somehow explains everything.

'Well, good luck,' he grins. 'You'll need it out there.' Instead of spending the afternoon in search of the boat bilge pump, Stu and I decide hunting the nearest pub down might do our spirits infinitely more good. Our passage up the Severn Estuary is booked for first light the next morning.

39

SEA

I've invited Helen's husband Andy and their son along for the trip too. I know from our conversations in Stratford that, like the marathon, it's a narrow-boating challenge he's wanted to complete for some time. They arrive early evening with fish and chips and a bottle of Helen's hedgerow-foraged home liqueur. It's powerful stuff. We consider dropping a little into the fuel tank to speed our progress tomorrow.

Sitting in a perfect camp circle in the kids' corner, two torches trained on the ceiling as most of the boat's bulbs need replacing by now, we assess Joseph's chances on the high seas. The Severn Estuary has the largest tidal range in Europe — over 10.5 metres at Sharpness and nearly 15 metres at Avonmouth — and stream velocities of up to eight knots. It's generally not recommended for inland waterway craft, particularly flat-bottomed narrow boats like mine. They're inherently unstable on waves and, if we encounter a significant swell and the boat is pitching, there's a good chance the uncovered forward cockpit could become swamped as the drainage ports on most canal boats wouldn't be able to clear the water fast enough. Then there's that small tidal issue. Timing is everything. If we set out too early there may be too little water above the Severn Road Bridge and that carries the danger of touching the riverbed. In some cases, boats have been rolled over on the sandbanks between the bridge and Sharpness. More likely is that the boat will be 'bumped' further and further onto the bank, damaging the propeller and/or rudder in the process. If we're too late, Sharpness may have already closed their gates to protect shipping in the system at high water, and then we'd be stuck.

Mostly though, I'm worried that my improvised safety measures will be found out when they're most needed. I'm suddenly mortified that I still don't know how to turn the bilge pump on — yet too embarrassed nonetheless to ask Andy to help. Hours later, when everyone's snoring off the elderflower or rosehip or rhubarb booze, I fancy I can hear the oil dripping out of the tool-twisted filter and that our steering will seize as soon as we're through Portishead Lock. When I finally dream, it's of the first book I remember being read to me by my mother. The titular hero, Scuffy the Tugboat, bobs towards the bottom right corner of its front cover with his distinctive blue smokestack and tomato-red hull. I see him beaming. I see the assembled waterside chorus of animals grinning benignly too. I see the entire book as I remember — a delightful, watery thing of great adventure and happy homecoming, with only mild peril in places. I smile in my sleep.

But something changes. When I start scrutinising the scene more closely I read in Scuffy's nightmare-altered expression a phrase that has stuck with me from another great boating novel — Conrad's *Heart of Darkness*. With his brow creased into a frown, bags bigger than Ikea's under his eyes and pupils so dilated I can only assume LSD had entered the farm slurry feeding the river just off page, Scuffy channels Kurtz's famous last words. The rabbits look terrified, the owl has two cruel yellow eyes, the fish gape too: 'The horror! The horror!'

For those who haven't read *Scuffy the Tug-boat and His Adventures Down the River* by Gertrude Crampton, I am now loath to recommend it. I will, however, provide a brief synopsis. Scuffy is a plaything with ideas above his station. He lives in a toy-shop window display in front of a blonde doll whose hand position suggests she is holding in a wee, and adjacent to two wind-up gentlemen in black suits and bowler hats. Disturbingly, the superfluous head-wear (indoors!) appears to have unbalanced the man on the right, whom the illustrator has angled a millisecond away from a smashed face on the tabletop. Scuffy exclaims petulantly: 'I was meant for bigger things.' The brown teddy bear on the floor performs a Far Right salute.

The shop's proprietor, who is never named except in relation to his flamboyantly spotted neckwear, takes Scuffy home for his son to splash with in the bath. The bath, I can now appreciate, is a rather lovely roll-top sort — very desirable. Scuffy, the ass, is scornful though: 'A tub is no place for a red-painted tugboat. I was meant for bigger things.' So the next day the man with the polka-dot tie and his son take Scuffy sailing on a 'laughing brook' (my narcotics suspicion now confirmed) and, to the consternation of his foster family, he skips away downstream singing, 'This is the life for me.' His voyage takes him merrily past washerwomen and thirsty cows, small villages and great, bridged towns. Scuffy is happy and toots this repeatedly, which makes his later complaint of noise pollution upon reaching the harbour hugely hypocritical. The cars and cranes, horses stamping, porters shouting, and then the sight of the wide, open sea, all give our bobbing hero a serious case of the heebie-jeebies. He freaks outs with an ocean poeticism that could as easily describe the rising flood of our bile for him: 'There is no beginning and there is no end.' Longing now for the pricey bathroom ceramics of the toy oligarch and his son, they appear just in time to pluck him to safety from the end of a pier and return him to the tub at home. The end.

But not in my dream. Here, instead of the man with the polka-dot tie and his little boy, is Andrew and *his* son and Stu too. They fail to grab Scuffy who, now I come to think of it, looks less tomato-red and more Satanic-black. Looks like *Joseph*, in fact. The picture book rests idly on the green carpet of his roof but I see the title has been defaced and now reads *Mein Kampf* in wicked bold letters. At Joseph's tiller is a girl who appears a little like me, except someone has drawn a neat black moustache on her upper lip without her noticing. She is scared. I can see it in the widening of her eyes and how she's pulled her sleeve right down over her free hand. The other clutches the tiller and steers into the lazy yawn of an enormous wave, which swallows the entire Severn Road Bridge and, before its mouth closes completely, a tiny floating bookshop and an even smaller, screaming, owner.

When I wake I'm relieved to see flat water and clear skies. I laugh off the Scuffy scare and we start Joseph up and meet our pilot in the lock. He takes a long, hard look at the makeshift fenders on our starboard side before boarding and glancing down the other end. He is satisfied, I note with undue surprise, that the semi-skimmed buffers are *not* replicated on this side. And so we set off into a water as different from a canal's as day from night. It plays and kicks and makes us grin to see. 'Let me steer,' I beg the pilot, and for a few seconds I can feel how it twists beneath us and chases its tail. Standing out there, all fleeced by buoyancy aids, all wearing identical masks of wind, we feel finally like proper sailors. I have grouped at the back lots of times before, with friends and family and hitchhikers and all the fictional passengers I can't shake off. But we've never stood quite like this. All stiffened, all staring, like the moai statues of a strange new Easter Island. Only our pilot seems unaffected. When I go down to make tea, I put his in my favourite *Treasure Island* mug so he's not quite left out of our adventure. Maybe under all that impassiveness he appreciates this because, nearing Sharpness, he concedes Joseph is the fastest narrow boat to make this passage. I already know it. I've been listening. He has pounded and thundered beneath us all this time.

40

LOW-LIFE

I don't really want to be on the canals after that. Not for the next three weeks at least. When I was much younger and before I learned how to swim properly, I used to ask my mother to blow up armbands and fit them on the little half-globes of my biceps. There was one of those long straight borders across each one, a boundary peculiar to the African continent whose map, especially in the north, looked like countries had been formed neatly, with a ruler and pencil, rather than through wars and bloodshed. The latitude on my arm delineated which part of the limb saw sun, and which stayed snowy white all year round under the loose sky of a Disney T-shirt or the capped sleeve of my school uniform. My armbands always rested on this line, half over tan, half over pale, scrupulously fair. With them fitted I'd turn my back to the pool, hold the railings of the ladder in and descend gingerly, letting out a shriek when the cold reached the costume between my legs. From here, while my elder siblings swam lengths and dive-bombed around me, I'd grip the red tiles that surrounded the pool and pull myself around its entire perimeter, over and over and over. Later, when I was brave enough to let go and trust those airy hillocks on my upper arms to hold me above the waterline, I hated going back to those sides, the no-man's-land between my parents' half-caught conversations from the sunbeds and the thrills of tumble-turning and ankle-grabbing with my sisters and brother. Going back to the canal is renouncing these pleasures. It is a slow, hand-by-hand nursery again. It is going back to the Midlands.

I sell books in Gloucester and Worcester, Stourport, Kinver, Norbury Junction and Market Drayton. Then I go into Wales on the Llangollen Canal. I cruise over the famous Pontcysyllte Aqueduct, the longest and highest in Britain. But even then, even with no edge but the iron plates beneath my feet, I don't feel the sweep that the Severn Estuary gave nor the boldness that filled me in Bristol. These weeks are a strange place to be, emotionally, geographically. I'm within an hour from home but not close enough to visit easily and not much wanting to either. I feel like I'm skirting around the place, some sort of outlawed pack animal, crouched, belly almost scraping the floor, like my boat. I start getting annoyed when people stop me now at locks to tell me the bookshop is a singular idea, which I had previously accepted as praise. I snap when customers suggest I might be lonely doing this by myself for six months. But when friends or family pay a visit I find there is nothing I can talk about but the boat and the books. I don't care for what's happening outside of this bubble and I like it best when they leave.

It's around this time that I start getting a strange series of prank calls and texts. My phone will ring at 3 a.m. with mobile numbers I don't recognise. Or I'll receive a message late evening as I'm preparing for bed, with a bad rhyme, the sort you'd find in a cheap valentine card. These I can deal with. I put my phone on silent when I sleep and delete the texts as they come in. But there are also ones that hint I know the sender, and these make me uneasy. They mention specifics of inside the boat and what I look like. They intimate we've had some kind of relationship — and recently — with cryptic phrases like: I'll never forget the night we spent together, or, I miss the touch of your fingers. These, when I wake in the night and read them, make me feel vulnerable for the first time since that horrible gunman dream. I'm reluctant to turn my mobile off completely in case I need it for an emergency. But, even with the message tone muted, I know one is there from the intermittent flashing of my screen warning me surer than a lighthouse beam of something ugly hidden in the dark. I start sleeping badly — and also doing something I haven't since childhood, which maybe terrifies me more. I get up from under my blankets, still unconscious, and wander over to the windows. I open the thin rectangular pane at the top. It swings inwards only wide enough to fit an arm through. I do that. I wake, usually from the cold, to see my fingers splayed on the opposite side of the glass trying to pull the rest of me through after them. Another night I wake in my sleeping bag. I'm hot, sweating. I turn on a torch to discover the reason is that I'm outfitted head to toe in waterproofs. My hands are dirty and there's mud on my feet too. In the morning I see that the mooring lines have been retied overnight. I have made three pretty bows of them in my sleep.

By now I've reached over halfway on this trip and people start asking what I'll do when I come home, which I don't know. I'm not sure exactly when the idea of taking The Book Barge to Paris entered my head, certainly long before this. I'd seen a boat moored in London that had made the crossing. It was a floating circus. A big trapeze folded up from its roof and girls put on shows for towpath audiences. Maybe then the seed was sown to make the opposite journey but I didn't give it too much thought. Cruising up the Bristol Channel brought the crazy scheme back to the fore of my thoughts. I remember asking for the pilot's contact details, only half in jest, so I could get in touch next year to engage his services across an infinitely scarier shipping lane to Calais. He'd laughed in my face.

Now, however, with the canal turning to autumn and my spirits all mixed up with the falling leaves, it starts to obsess me in a new way. I have a kids' Paris map laid out on my desk most evenings when I'm done moving for the day. It's a bright, silly thing. Nothing is to scale. Cars drive upside down on the Avenue de la Republique and a big red coffee cup north-east of the Gare du Nord dwarfs the TGV zooming underneath its saucer. On the Bateaux-Mouches two people wave their arms and shout something I can't quite hear, while a black cat stalks towards Pont Neuf. The Sorbonne wears Harry Potter glasses. This is the city I imagine squeezing my bookshop into. At the tiller in driving rain the next day I speak schoolroom French aloud to all the interesting made-up customers who come down the steps of my dream boat. Our conversations veer towards the restaurant vocabulary I'm most familiar with so, after greeting the book browser politely and asking if they have any siblings or pets, I end up announcing 'j'espère fermer le magasin pour cinq minutes' and inviting them to join me for a ham sandwich and 'jus d'orange' instead. What a lovely working life it'll be there, I sigh. All easy café talk and no credit card repayment quarrels.

Now when *real* people ask my future plans I'm straight in with the Gallic grand tour. 'After spending the summer on the Canal Saint-Martin, I'll probably cruise around the rest of the country for a while,' I say breezily.

'Sounds wonderful,' they enthuse, 'why not write a book?'

'Why not indeed,' I pretend yawn. 'I'll call it L'Eau Life,' like I've just thought that title up and not been waiting a fortnight to shoehorn it into a conversation. And then I show them shelves newly stocked with Francophile titles, which are feeding my dreams. There's *French Women Don't Get Fat* and *French Children Don't Throw Food* and, my particular favourite at this time, the aspirational *Parisian Chic: A Style Guide* by the model Inès de la Fressange. Just holding its chic red cover flexi-bound with a wrapper band and aquarelle paper makes me feel a little bit closer to timeless allure and effortless glamour. This is in fact what the book promises for the reasonable RRP of £19.95.

Somewhere south of Middlewich I get upset to read that elasticated legwear is a French wardrobe faux pas and exchange the book for five packets of crisps and a Chomp at my earliest convenience, which is in the outskirts of Sale. I give the ten-year-old girl no other choice of literature. She will grow up stylish and grateful, partnering chiffon print dresses with battered biker boots, tux jackets with sneakers and never resting until she's been to the City of Love *en personne* to fetch her own Eric Bompard navy V-necked sweater.

41

LOVE LIFE (part i)

I meet a man with a tarot deck. 'You're on a journey,' he says. I can't suppress a cynical snort. 'Shut up,' he says, 'I'm just telling you what the cards say. You're on a journey', he begins again, 'and you're doing it because you believe everyone at home thinks you're a failure.' Ouch. I sit up straighter at this point and put down my whiskey. His cat jumps onto my lap and purrs over the cards too. He continues. 'In the past, you've been governed by impulse and maybe don't think things through.' There's a queen figure he mentions, who sounds pretty feminist and fun and he talks about her for a while too.

'What about the future though?' I ask. 'What's in store?'

'You'll take a more considered approach to life. See this card here? It represents science, rationality.'

'Everything I'm not?' I volunteer.

'You'll pay more attention to it in future,' he insists.

'Great. Sounds a blast,' I say. I lean back

and down the rest of the Jack Daniels.

'There are two men,' he starts up again, 'the Prince of Discs and the Prince of Wands.'

'They sound dreamy,' I enthuse. 'Rich? Handsome? Potential Book Barge investors? French aristocracy?'

'I can't help you with specifics,' he sighs, 'remember what I told you about tarot reading?'

'Yes,' I nod like a good student, 'the cards can't predict the events of your life, they can only help you make sense of it as you live it.'

'Correct.' He's pleased. 'I can only offer suggestions,' he says. 'You do the reading yourself. Like with books. You pick up on the passages most pertinent to you. You gloss over those that have no relevance.' He pours more whiskey and sits there thoughtfully a while.

'Can we do one on your cat?' I ask.

I meet him halfway through my Midlands depression/Paris hype. He and his wife invite me onto their boat for dinner and a shower as I'm cruising past. It's too good an offer to turn down so I moor up immediately and am drinking wine and drying my hair in front of their wood burner twenty minutes later. I like them both a lot. We chat until late and then the man offers to carry on down the canal a short way with me the next day to help with locks. I like them infinitely more. Except,

213

despite getting up and knocking on their hatch early, as agreed, it's now 10am and the tarot deck and whiskey have been out for two hours and there's no sign yet of moving on.

'Tell me more about my princes,' I beg as soon as we've implied the cat's fate (crusades, valour, kittens and duck liver). But he's adamant that love is a mystery and I'll only know them when they present themselves. 'Is one a businessman and one a gardener?'

'Sounds an unlikely ménage à trois,' he laughs, 'but if you can make the shoe fit?' I can't, whichever way I try. So we talk about his life instead, beginning with his crazy first marriage to a complete stranger after being imprisoned by his ex-girlfriend for weeks and force-fed hallucinogenics. I make him tell me this story twice it's so good. And then he talks about his current marriage, which has been a happy one, but how he wants to escape from time to time and take a boat right out to sea and around the world. 'You and everyone else,' I sympathise. And when we finally get the engine going he tells me there's only one thing I need to know about love, and that's that it should make me sing. So right there and then he breaks into Fathom the Bowl, a stupid sea shanty, and makes me do the chorus in my best gravelly baritone until, for the first time in weeks, I'm halfway back to happy again. *We'll fathom the bowl, we'll fathom the bowl, bring the punch ladle, we'll fathom the bowl.*

42

LOVE LIFE (part ii)

A girl I used to work with in my first job, at a paparazzi agency in London, joins me on the boat for three days. For half of this time she reads aloud an entire *Women's Weekly* library novella. We're not particularly close friends, although we've been on holiday together once in the past. The story she chooses is a random one from a small stack I sell for 20p each on the boat. They are popular for their retro covers and cool misogyny, which makes girls gasp in places, as it does me when my friend is reading our story. She reads aloud to pass the time. She reads aloud because we had a small argument over turning the engine on to charge her iPhone the night before. She reads aloud because I beg her not to stop. It's the worst sort of romance story but she reads it until her voice gives up and I have to run inside to find more red wine for her to soothe it. She reads it by torchlight before we go to sleep. She reads it all the next morning too. By the time she finishes I know something new about love. I know that, every so often, it can surprise us how much of it we feel for our friends.

43

LOVE LIFE (part iii)

My university lecturer said, 'If you want to know about love, you've got to study the metaphysical poets.' So we started with John Donne.

This is what John Donne told me about love then:

- The exploration of America = the act of fondling
- A flea biting two lovers = sex
- The Hellespont = the gap between a lover's breasts

I thought puh-lease. But I wrote something more articulate in my exam.

This is what John Donne tells me about love now:

John Donne wrote a poem called *A Valediction: Forbidding Mourning*. A valediction is an expression we use to say goodbye, like those set phrases we end a letter or email with. Except Donne's not much of a fan of the 'Regards' or 'Cheers' or 'Peace' or

'TTFN'. He prefers something a little lengthier. His valediction is thirty-six lines. In it he tells his lover that, despite his absence, their relationship will be fine. To be more precise, he says:

– A pair of compasses = you and me apart

But this comparison doesn't make me gag. Donne says his lover is like the 'fixt foot' that 'when the other far doth rome, . . . leanes, and hearkens after it, / And growes erect, as that comes home.' This makes me think of Stu. It makes me think of when we first met and I was going to West Africa for a few months because I'd arranged it all before I even knew him. So he made me a box and he covered it with jungle wrapping paper. Inside he put three potatoes, a Bic biro with blue ink, a notebook, squits tablets, Dove soap and vitamin pills with the mathematics attached of how to ration them during my time there. And there were 'specially selected items of clothing' so I wouldn't stick out like a foreigner, including 'two especially crap hats' of which the first was a Talyllyn Railway one and the other a camouflage print. And I went — and I came back to him. Before university he gave me a similar survival pack in a school satchel covered in pin badges and an

Incredible Hulk lunchbox. And I went — and I came back to him. Then I moved to London — and I moved back *with* him two years later. Donne says: 'Thy firmness drawes my circle just, / And makes me end, where I begunne.'

When I walked away from him, Stu only gave me the black bin liner I'd packed my clothes into. I look at where I've been so far with the boat, and all the canals up North I've still to get through. I use a blue biro to mark the entire course. It makes a poor sort of shape. It wavers right from the start. It goes back on itself in places, it falters constantly. It's a tatty, raggedy circle, if it can even be called that. I fancy it makes the outline of a remote island.

Donne's other lesson is that 'No man is an island'. But my evidence stands: I am cartographer and castaway. I claim the territory with a black flag and the great poet's own pun: I am Un-Donne.

44

LOVE LIFE (part iv)

I'm on the boat with my school friend, Katie, when two teenage boys whistle for our attention from the towpath.

Boy 1: Show us the way to Oldham?
Me: To Oldham? Um, that way, I think (points in the direction we've travelled from).
Boy 1: Nooooo. This is the way to old 'em! (cups a pair of imaginary tits on Boy 2).
Me: . . . .
Boy 1: Hahahahahahahahahahahaha
Katie: . . . .
Boy 2: Hahahahahahahahahahahaha

45

BLISS

Coming into Manchester you go right past Old Trafford — the Theatre of Dreams, they call it. It's a match night and there are pockets of people outside and hanging over the bridge waiting. A few of them wave as I cruise under so I shout back good luck, which makes them cheer and knock bottles together. The glass on glass makes a pretty sound. It peals with me under the Trafford Road Bridges and through the pigeon breath of the dark railway arches too. I see a jogger there paused for breath, his back and head folded down towards his knees. Hearing the engine, he snaps upright like all those sprung stadium seats and he starts his run again.

I moor in Castle Quay by a radio station and a couple of smart restaurants. Even though it's the start of October there's a brief heatwave and business is good. A folk band plays on the bow of the boat and three authors are lined up for signings. The Midlands and Wales had seen a dearth of book swaps — on occasions it had felt more like begging — but here in Manchester a finely balanced interdependency is back. There's also real support for the wider motivation for this trip — to put the spotlight on independent bookshops in general, not just this one. Customers tell me about the ones they miss in Manchester and they blog enthusiastically about mine. They call up their mates from outside the boat, or Tweet pictures of the shelves. They find out where else I'll be stopping in the next month and hook me up with family and friends they have in those places.

Yes, The Book Barge is spoilt here. Every now and then I leave the shop unattended and run up the steps of the white footbridge above it, sometimes with my camera, sometimes just my curiosity. I fix my elbows to the railing, rest my head on the girder of my open palms and watch delightedly as people walk in and step out, or bend to look through the windows, or take a book out front to read in the sun. I'll settle for much less too: a quick glance thrown by a man in a dark suit, late to work on his phone; a child bouncing a tennis ball off its steel shoulder; an old man holding onto the lip of the roof to steady himself while he shakes a stone from his sandal. It's acknowledgement, a small connection. I feel it as a bite of pride.

That someone else could ever share a similar sentiment about the boat never crossed my mind until Manchester. A woman called Claire came aboard a couple of days after I arrived. She asked questions about the shop, about me, and was equally forthcoming about her own life and her experiences with books. She invited me to a literary event she was taking part in later that day, which I couldn't attend because of a prior engagement, and which I regretted. She bought two books and when she left I felt a strange sadness because I would probably never get to know her better or become her friend. A few days later someone directed me to a complimentary blogpost that had been written about the shop. It was by the same woman — I recognised her name. I was grateful for all the kind stuff in there but a bit at the end made me stop dead. It was a description of how she felt after she left the shop. She used a quote from a short story she had bought here, one called *Bliss* by Katherine Mansfield. This is what it said:

Although Bertha Young was thirty she still had moments like this when she wanted to run instead of walk, to take dancing steps on and off the pavement, to bowl a hoop, to throw something up in the air and catch it again, or to stand still and laugh at — nothing

224

— at nothing, simply.

What can you do if you are thirty and, turning the corner of your own street, you are overcome, suddenly, by a feeling of bliss — absolute bliss! — as though you'd suddenly swallowed a bright piece of that afternoon sun and it burned in your bosom, sending out a little shower of sparks into every particle, into every finger and toe?

That meant a lot to me. Sometimes, if you work for yourself and by yourself, the hardest thing is not having someone to share good moments with, as well as the rubbish things. The Mansfield quote was the closest anyone has ever come to articulating the best bits of my job, the senseless joy it can shoot through me in the throwaway comment of a happy customer or in the way the ropes keen at night. Sometimes I get giddy just watching the twitching light show the water throws onto the ceiling or when you catch the expression of a passenger in a car nodding over the bridge you're approaching, and it's one of longing.

If Mansfield calls this feeling bliss, who am I to argue? I never thought I'd get it from a sixty-foot canal boat on a tiny arm of the industrial Bridgewater Canal. It's more than that though — it's a kind of confidence, one that I never knew I had. A couple of weeks later I read another author, Haruki Murakami, giving voice to what makes him feel that way in an article in the *Guardian*. He's talking about his childhood, how he grew up knowing he could never match the expectations his parents harboured for him and how he sensed their disappointment, even from an early age. How did you find the confidence then to do what you wanted? the interviewer asks. And Murakami replies that he always had it because he always knew what he loved. He lists reading, listening to music and cats. He says, 'I know what I love, still, now. That's a confidence.' I think of my boat and my books. Yes, I love them. And a third thing, a person, who also once loved me back.

46

BLUE

There's not much call for this way of thinking on the Leeds & Liverpool Canal. It's graft and tears and a whole lot of grief from a woman outside Keighley. More on her later. I'm in a hurry.

In fact, it seems I'm always in a rush on this trip. My six-month allowance to get around the country is obviously more generous than Phileas Fogg's eighty-day global quota, yet I'm unable to replicate the gentleman traveller's bewildering calm and exactitude. Cruising days are long, increasingly fraught affairs. It can often take an entire week to get between big towns where trade is likely to be busiest. Between them I'm not usually taking any money at all. Perhaps it's this thought, shared by the hapless Passepartout who left the gas 'remorselessly burning at his expense in Saville Row', which has something to do with our 'hot impatience'.

I love *Around the World in 80 Days*. Jules Verne nicknamed it 'the novel of perpetual motion'. Before picking up his pen to write, he first sketched the figures of Fogg and Passepartout, cut them out in cardboard and routed them across the three oceans and four continents of his novel by impaling their bodies with hat pins on a wall map. (I'm thrilled, when I get home from my trip, to discover my parents have made a similar chart of The Book Barge's progress. There's no boat fashioned from a cereal box and Blu-tacked to its centre, but there are dates and arrows and other scrawls that make it look like there was a method to the madness, a carefully plotted narrative.)

It's on the Leeds & Liverpool Canal that I first appreciate why Verne had his wagering hero insist on bringing a valet. There's the small topographical detail of the Pennines dividing the two cities that give the waterway its name. And with hills come locks. Lots of them. In my canal guide they're marked by little black arrowheads, like so many comically raised eyebrows. They're monstrous things. At Wigan there's a flight of twenty-one. I complete half on my own before running aground in one of the longer pounds between two and having to sit and wait for another boat, also coming up, to walk ahead, wind up paddles and send extra water coursing down to refloat me. After that I stick close to this boat and we do the rest together. A middle-aged man and teenaged boy work the gates and paddles with me. Inside their boat are two more people, but they stay in front of a TV screen and I don't meet them until we fall into the pub together at the top. It's here that I learn to stop feeling sorry for myself. The older man introduces me to the other two passengers, his adopted children, both severely mentally and physically handicapped. The lad who was helping him is his biological daughter's boyfriend. The man tells how caring for this family is a full-time job. It sounds exhausting. This is my first holiday in five years, he tells me. He is mopping up one of the kids' vomit as he says this. I want to ask how this — the locks, the responsibility of three kids, the extra challenges of two being disabled, the rain throwing darts at the window behind us — constitutes a holiday. But I daren't. I take up the cow-shaped milk jug that one of the boys has poured a blue alcopop into and decant it back into the bottle. It's an odd sight — the blue jet spouting from a porcelain cow's mouth. The boy asks me to do it again. 'This is milk,' he keeps insisting.

'No. Not milk.' But in the end I give in. 'OK, blue milk.' His father starts laughing and it spreads quick. My arm shakes from it as I pour for the last time.

'I dunno,' he says, as if he somehow heard the question I was too afraid to ask, 'maybe we're all a bit delusional.'

By the time I hit Blackburn, I'm ready to give up. I've spent a sleepless night listening to a gang of youths with spray cans outside. I'm sure they're aiming at Joseph's staid black coat and I'm sure the result won't be a Banksy either. I'm wrong. In the morning he's still pristine but for the old scribbles of rust and mud. On the wall opposite him I read that Keri and Adam have consummated their relationship and that Ellie is considered obese and a 'c' word amongst her peer group. I call Graeme to beg for a day's help.

Graeme is the finest Passepartout a traveller against the clock could wish for. That day we do thirteen locks and run a red light on the entrance to the 1640-yard long Foulridge Tunnel to reach the pub on the other side just half an hour after nightfall. On the way we successfully navigate over a sofa in Burnley and get to the bottom of the business of why the propeller has stopped turning. 'It's a head, it's a *human head*,' I wail, one arm in the weed hatch, the other grabbing his ankle to haul myself up. We look at each other solemnly.

'Are you *sure* it's a head you felt?' he asks

me, slowly putting on the long, red rubber glove to investigate for himself.

'Definitely. My finger went *down its ear*,' I sob. Graeme whitens but crouches down to cop a feel for himself.

'So . . . a head, hey?' he says, ten minutes of tussling with the propeller later. I look down at the fifteen metres of blue electrical cable and assorted women's hosiery he's untangled and pulled out.

'There was *almost certainly* a nose,' I maintain thinly.

It's because of the selflessness of people like Graeme and the guy in Blackburn that the horrible business with the Keighley woman kicks off. I have been struggling all morning through a succession of swing bridges. Let me tell you about swing bridges. They're little shits. If you're single-handed, the almost insurmountable problem is how to open it and get back on your boat when the pivot and the vessel are on opposite sides of the water. The logic of swing bridges relies on a boat having at least two crew members. One will stay on and cruise through once passage is clear. The other will hop off just before the bridge, scamper across, unlock it, haul it open, wait for the boat to come through, close it, lock it, and trot back over the bridge to be picked up from the towpath by the (hopefully) waiting boat. On your own, this pretty little picture of canalside industriousness breaks down rather. Or, in my case, turns into carnage.

Now in some instances it's just about possible to moor on the non-towpath side of the canal. You simply (simply!) point the boat's nose towards the bridge's pivot, flick into neutral to lose some speed, run through the boat, grab the bow line, make a flying leap into hedgerow and tie to a tree stump while you swing open the bridge. Then you tug the boat through, invariably fall in, grab a stern line once it's clear, keep hold of it in your teeth while you're closing the bridge, and then clamber back on. This effortless manoeuvre presupposes that it's *just* nettles and swamp you're up against on the far bank. If there's a brick wall, barbed wire, private property sign, Dobermann or any other obstacle to a smooth triple jump landing you're buggered.

In the case of the Keighley woman, it was just the middle two that were giving slight cause for concern. I was attempting my fourth bow line vault when I spied her walking up the towpath, a plastic kerchief over her curiously oranged hair to protect against the drizzle and a bag of groceries in each hand. To me, just at that moment, she

232

was an angel. 'Ahoy,' I called, 'you couldn't help me for just a second could you?' She stopped and fixed her eyes on mine like two leeches.

'What exactly would you have me do?' she queried.

'Oh, it's easy. Just swing the bridge open on the other side while I go through and close it again after.' She put down her shopping bags and I ran back through the boat to the tiller, praising gods and believing in miracles. But when I'd pushed myself off with a barge pole and reversed back into the middle of the channel, it gave me a fright to see her standing, not on the bridge, but immediately to my right, with the thunderous skies of Yorkshire reflected in her darkened face.

'Young. Lady.' she spat. 'How. Very. Dare. You.'

47

MUTTON

Hell hath no fury like a Keighley woman asked to open a swing bridge. It's lessons like these that a career in floating bookselling can teach a girl. And it's an important one. Without, it's possible you might live out your years believing that canals are quaint, innocuous things. That boaters and passers-by live peaceably side by side. That sheep, those warts of our fields, are dumb, harmless beasts and in no way complicit in the atrocity that follows.

I initially think that the woman must have misheard me. 'I'm sorry,' I say, 'we've got our wires crossed. I just wanted you to pull open the bridge for me so I can pass through. It's very difficult on my own.' She stamps her booted foot irritably.

'I *did* hear you,' she says. 'And I think it's disgusting — *disgusting* — of you to ask such a thing of a small, frail old lady.' I look around quickly for the small, frail old lady before realising she's referring to the clod of early middle-aged, dale-thickened muscle mass in front of me.

'Ohhhhh, okay. Look, don't worry then. I'll keep trying on my own. Have a nice day.' And I get back to it.

But the woman won't move. She stands as I left her, hands on hips, shaking her head and, every now and then, thudding her heels petulantly into the mud. A sheep peers over the stone wall behind her to investigate the strange hissing noise she's emitting from the left corner of her mouth when she gives another hard stomp, which makes the animal fall clear over the wall and onto the towpath in fright. Sheep being sheep (asses) two more swoon over the same wall after her so now I've got a splenetic woman from Keighley and three specimens of livestock all goggling from the side while I'm one foot aboard the boat, one foot all caught up in the barbed wire and I'm feeling my patience running out. 'Hey, if you're not going to help there's not much point hanging around watching me,' I yell to the woman, 'I'll be here a while.'

So the woman plods off but the sheep remain transfixed and I start shouting at them too. I've heard weird things about the sheep up here. Locals claim they're cleverer than the ones down south, that they can demonstrate problem-solving abilities. What I've heard is that they've found a way to cross cattle grids by rolling on their backs like commandos. Looking at these three with their snide grins and their slow chewing I can believe it. I splash up the water with my useless steel-knotted leg to spook them but the one furthest from me just airbags them all off the wall and back onto their toes when they buckle. And then from down the towpath I can hear the woman coming back screeching, 'What are you doing to those poor animals, WHAT ARE YOU DOING?'

'They were looking at me funny,' I scream back.

'Well, wouldn't anyone,' she sniffs: 'Look at your boat. What is it anyway?'

'It's a *bookshop*,' I seethe.

'Yes, of course it is,' and she's marching away again shaking her head.

I give up then. I reverse the boat back to the towpath side, tie up and sit in the mud letting the sheep spit into my hood and laugh in my face. 'You're all bastards,' I tell them. 'And it's the last time I'm doing the decent thing by one of your drowned comrades,' for I've been interrupting my journey across the country to bail out their bloated bodies and give them a decent funeral under hedges wherever I can. And sheep corpses stink and are heavy. So that's the last time. I can spy the woman sitting on a bench further along the towpath, still keeping an eye on proceedings: Her white shopping bags either side sandwich her like the patty she is. Only now can I appreciate the tactics of an old man I once shared a lock with on the Kennet & Avon. He had stretched his mooring lines across the towpath into the low-hanging branches of a tree while he was waiting for the lock to empty. A cyclist had blurred past my boat, which was waiting behind him, and straight into the trap. It caught the head tube and threw the rider clean over the handle-bars. I had been shocked by the incident. An argument had followed between the old man and the cyclist, where the old man had refused to apologise. 'It's *our* canal,' he kept saying, including me in his crazed imperial-ism with a sweep of his arm. 'Water's for boaters, roads are for botherers,' he con-cluded triumphantly.

I'm ready now to join him in quashing the infidels. Let's joust them off their pushbikes with our barge poles, create wide wakes to purge the banks of fishermen, lay land mines of dog turd to deter ramblers and erect tall gun turrets above our hatchways to take out gongoozlers with our mouldy clementines. I'm ready to die on the next lock gate waving a red flag and belting out *Les Mis* show tunes. Good god: I realise, suddenly appalled at my bloodthirst, that I've become a *narrow boater*.

It's thirty-five minutes before a young couple walk past with a pushchair and open the bridge for me. The woman on the bench is long gone. While I'd hidden my head in my hands, sobbing over the monster the inland waterways had made of me, she had walked back over and tapped my shoulder sharply. The sheep, in their infinite Yorkshire wisdom, scarpered at this point. My eyes were too blurred by tears to note if they'd pole-vaulted the wall back into their field or merely fallen over it the way they came out. But the watery vision made the woman from Keighley appear softer. Her orange lipstick looked less toxic, more like a boiled baby carrot swimming in the pudding of her face. When she opened that mouth though, the wrath that came out was a bitter gravy. 'I DON'T GET IT,' she steamed. She crouched down to chump her fingers tight around my arm. 'JUST. GET. A. BUS. INSTEAD.'

48

JOSEPH

There's a Lyle Lovett song about simultaneously wanting a pony and a boat. I've never heard it sung but some of the lyrics are quoted in a book about Hemingway I read once. The song suggests it's not such a crazy thing to wish for both a horse and a boat. If you luck out and get the pair, it goes, you can just saddle up and cast off and sit, happy as a dream, upon the steed upon the deck upon the sea. I put the words to my own tune and we carry on, Joseph and I. We cinch in a little more of the brown belt that waists our island. I talk to the boat now more than ever. He listens well and holds those secrets dry in the shallow tub under his floorboards. In between I collect the names of all the boats we go past, just as I used to alphabetise horses' ones in the Body Shop spiral-bound notebook that was a Christmas present a long time ago. They're disappointing usually — Narrow Escape, Tranquility, Dreamcatcher, Willow, Moor to Life, Lucky Duck, Tardis — but I say them aloud anyway and run the list of the day's so far back and forth on my tongue until I stumble over Pendragon or Iron Maiden or forget Cirrhosis of the River and then I start again.

Joseph keeps his head down and the canal A-lines from his nose. He has a peculiar grace for a narrow boat. With little in the way of furniture inside he sits high in the water so I can fancy he prances down the cut. The tiller bar is loose after all this time and the tremors it sends up my arm adds to the strange nervous energy of our cruises lately. He has been mine for almost three years now but it's only recently that I've appreciated the jaunty angle of his headlights or the warm breath of exhaust that I dangle my toes over. I'm haphazard with tightening the stern gland greaser or checking oil and water levels but he doesn't punish me for the neglect. I've rarely sponged his paintwork and still haven't replaced those fenders. He wears his dust and scrapes like a favourite hoodie, I fancy. There's a term fishermen use to describe a boat that performs as reliably in rough oceans as calm waters and that's 'sea-kindly'. Though the canal doesn't throw up much in the way of rolling waves and sneaky currents, I've come to rely on Joseph starting first time on cold mornings and running smooth all day with the hot palms of the sun pressing on his metal. And I call that a kindness too.

240

Today we're heading for Saltaire, a carefully planned community built in the mid- to late-1800s by manufacturer and philanthropist Titus Salt to house his mill workers. For all the wonderful social improvements Salt made, he also had sympathies for the temperance movement and imposed a ban on 'beer shops' in the village to stave off the evils of drink. This history is weighing on my mind a little because I've agreed to host a local book group there whose name is Reading Between the Wines.

★　★　★

I remember the first time I thought books might offer something more than plain escapism. I'm in English and, after weeks of supply teachers and copying notes from an overhead projector in silence, we have a new teacher called Mr Johnson and he's reading aloud from the start of our next set text, *The Mayor of Casterbridge*. 'What does fustian mean?' someone asks, about the description Thomas Hardy gives of the hero's waistcoat. I am hardly listening. A few pages later: 'What's furmity, Sir?' about the rum-laced porridge he's getting drunk on. The interruptions are making it difficult to sustain the fantasy that Graeme Smith, who sits behind me next period in geography, will ask me out. The futility of this hope (one, my NHS glasses have only recently made the fashion leap from pink hexagonal plastic to baroque titanium ovals; two, I've not actually heard Graeme Smith speak — to anyone) add to the daydream's swift extinction. I start paying reluctant attention to the story.

As all good GCSE students will tell you, *The Mayor of Casterbridge* is about an unfortunate hay trusser who, after guzzling too much alcoholic Ready Brek, flogs his wife and, after the passing of some years and events, dies pretty much alone. The will he pins above his deathbed is godawfully depressing on first read. Having gone on to study Hardy's other works, it becomes retrospectively chipper. It was set in the same period Titus Salt was deliberating teetotal town planning and, if we're to assume spousal retail when sozzled on rum was not an isolated incidence, Saltaire's sobriety may have a point.

But it was precisely this literary bender that got me seriously hooked on books. When Michael Henchard, his wife and their young child are introduced in Chapter One, the perfect silence they preserve is mentioned over and over. Horribly self-conscious as a teenager and oppressively shy around strangers, I was only just beginning to realise what a blessing alcohol can be to introverts. So I was fascinated to see the change rum makes in Henchard — how his conversation, previously so callipered, makes great delighted strides across the furmity tent. Sitting in that English lesson, I imagined my own leviathan tongue loosen and nimble, a sea of faces saucered to catch my spilling words.

I went home from school that day and carried on reading — but differently. Later I would realise it wasn't the drink talking to me in that scene, it was the other words too: that amazing description of the auctioneer (the 'short man, with a nose resembling a copper knob, a damp voice, and eyes like button-holes'), the detail of the swallow and its 'quick curves' that briefly interrupts proceedings. I had always enjoyed books but now they became more important. They articulated things I was never very good at voicing. They were conversations I could take part in.

★ ★ ★

We're in the last lock before Saltaire, Hirst's Lock. It's ten foot two inches deep and has a leaky back gate, which isn't a euphemism for anything other than the horrible fact that the water it's throwing in is about to flood my boat. I'm maybe tired after the early start, maybe paying less attention than normal because I'm so close to our destination for the night. Whatever the reason, I can see the water spraying onto the back of Joseph as the lock level goes down but I don't start to worry much until I see a small straw rectangle floating down the side of the boat and realise it's the door mat from the top of the stairs. The water inside the lock has now almost dropped to the level of the canal in front so I figure the most practical thing is to open one of the gates, run down the ladder and then steer out and assess the damage once we're clear of the flow from the rear gate. Except, once I'm on the boat and ready to manoeuvre out I realise how silent it is down here, apart obviously from the water throwing onto our backs. The key's still turned in the ignition but I can't hear the engine and I know then that something hideous has happened and I'll have to pull the boat out with ropes. All this time the water keeps beating us and beating us and when I peek under the cover of the engine compartment it's already a swimming pool down there.

On any other canal, hauling the boat from the lock wouldn't have posed too much of a problem. The Leeds & Liverpool is different though. The locks are shorter — sixty feet — the exact length of Joseph. As such, the boat has got wedged behind the closed gate and, above the lock once more, I realise I'll need an extra pair of hands to pull the stern over while I simultaneously push off the bow with my legs. I fly down the ladder again to try to at least shuffle the stern out of the direct flow of water but I can't shift it.

It's then that I notice the face of a primary school girl peering down into the lock. Before I can call out, she disappears. Seconds later her face is back, and this time with an older sister, maybe eight or nine. Please, please, please make them be too young to be walking home from school unsupervised. 'GET YOUR PARENT,' I scream, and they run off again. They reappear with their father.

It's a mess. Tied up now on the rings just outside the lock I start bailing the water from around the engine with a plant pot. The family who helped get me out have gone home. I'm still probably half an hour's cruising from Saltaire, too far to pull the boat by hand. I need to keep bailing and hope, once the water's down, the engine will cough out its canal-phlegmed lungs and get moving again for me. 'Joseph,' I say, full realising I'm the most pathetic being ever to have loved an inanimate hulk of steel, bookshelves, bad gardening and rusted flanks, 'please don't die.'

PART TWO

49

BLACKED BEAUTY

The first place that I can well remember was a large, pleasant mooring with an old wharf. Two willows overshadowed the canal, and ducks swam all around. Over the pontoon on one side we looked at a row of pub picnic tables; and on the other we looked up a slipway to the boat shed where I was made. If you followed the canal west, I was told you would reach the great River Mersey; and if you inclined in the other direction you would reach the running River Trent at Derwent Mouth.

While I was young I stayed a long time in the boat shed, as I was not yet watertight. In the daytime men would weld heavy steel sheets together to form my shell, and at night I would cool and sleep. As soon as I was old enough to float and my hull had been blacked, the men took me onto the water. They would work on cladding my interior with thin marine plywood, and go home to their families in the evening.

There were four boats in the canal besides

me. They were older than I was and different shapes. Two were small cabin cruisers; the other two were traditional working boats and so had a stern that was more enclosed than my cruiser style and black sheet tenting from cabin to fore deck. I used to bob with them and have great fun. We used to bob up and down, up and down, pulling our mooring lines as tight as they could go. Sometimes we had rather rough play, for they would frequently nudge and bump sides as well as head-butt the bank.

One day, when there was a good deal of shoving, a matronly duck quacked to me to come to her; and then she said: 'I wish you to pay attention to what I am going to say to you. The boats who live here are good boats, but they are working boats and day trippers, and, of course, they have not learned good manners.

'You have been well bred and well made. I hope you will grow up gentle and good, and never learn bad ways. Do your work with a good will; let your engine tick smoothly when you cruise and never nudge or bump even in play.'

I have never forgotten the duck's advice; I knew she was a wise old bird. Her name was Deirdre.

My master was a good, kind man. He gave

us good moorings and tied our lines firm; and he spoke as kindly to us as he did to his little children. We were all fond of him, and Deirdre loved him very much. When she saw him at the bank, she would quack with joy and swim up to him. He would throw her bread and say, 'Well, old duck! How is your little Darkie?' I was a dull black, so he called me Darkie.

Then he would give me a piece of bread, which was weird, and sometimes he brought a carrot for Deirdre, which she thought a little unorthodox too. All the ducks and boats would jostle for his attention, but I think Deirdre and I were his favourites. Deirdre sometimes laid him an egg, and he ate it even though his Daily Mail newspaper warned he may catch salmonella.

There was a chav, Kyle, who sometimes came along the tow-path on a scrambler motorbike and gave everyone a terrible fright. When he got bored of riding and practising lame tricks he would have, what he called, fun with the swans, throwing sticks and stones at them to make them hiss. We did not much mind him, for we were made of sterner stuff than feather; but sometimes a stone would hit us and smash a windowpane.

One day he was at this game, and did not know that the master was in the boat shed;

but he was there, watching what was going on. Down the slipway he ran in a moment, and catching Kyle by the arm, called the police on his mobile phone with his free hand. As soon as we saw the master, we bobbed nearer to see what was going on.

'Little bastard!' he said, 'Little bastard! to vandalise the boats. This is not the first time nor the second, but it shall be the last.' So we never saw Kyle again because the police slapped him with an ASBO.

Old Dave, the man who looked after the boats, was just as gentle as our master, so we were well off.

★   ★   ★

I was now beginning to grow handsome; my coat had been painted and polished, and was glossy black. I had two cream tunnel bands on my stern where other boats had red and white ones, and a pair of bow thrusters. People thought me very handsome.

When I was six months old, Squire Patrick came to look at me. He examined my engine and my bilge, and felt my hull all the way down to the waterline. Then I had to accelerate, reverse and bow thrust before him. He seemed to like me, and said, 'When he has been well broken in, he will do very well.' My master promised to break me in himself as he would not like me to be frightened or hurt; and he lost no time about it, for the next day the breaking-in began.

Everyone may not know what breaking in is, so I will describe it. To break in a canal boat is to teach it to carry on its back a man, woman, or child; to go just the way the captain wishes, and to do so without running aground or colliding with an oncoming vessel. Besides this, the boat must wear a tiller to be steered with; and he must learn to stand still when being filled with diesel.

Of course, I had long been used to keys in the ignition and a short cruise to the winding hole and back, but now I was to go through a lock.

My master gave me some acceleration as usual, and after a good deal of coaxing, he got me into the chamber. What a nasty thing the lock was! Those who have never been in one cannot know how bad it feels. A great piece of dark, slimy wood as thick as a man's thigh is closed behind you, with a similar gate blocking off escape in front; so that no way in the world can you get out of the nasty dirty thing. Then he must be taught how to pass through a lock; he must learn to go up with the water or down with the water, just as his captain wishes. He must never start at the torrent crashing around him; or grow impatient waiting for it to empty, even though he may be very tired or bored. He must avoid getting stuck on the cill at all times. Bad! bad! Yes, very bad! At least I thought so; but I knew the inland waterways are full of such horrors, and that all narrow boats face them when they go cruising. And so, what with my master's pats, kind words, and gentle ways, and not having any choice in the matter, I learnt how to face a lock.

I must not forget to mention one part of my training, which I have always considered a very great advantage. My master sent me for a fortnight to the other side of the canal, the towpath side, and moored me by the pub garden. Here were some members of the public, and I was turned in amongst them.

I shall never forget the first gongoozler to spot me. I was bobbing quietly near two moorhens, when I heard a strange sound at a distance; and before I knew whence it came — with a rush and a clatter, and a click-click-clicking of camera — a curiously bearded man jumped on my gunwales and started fondling my brass mushroom vent. I rocked him off onto the towpath and pulled away on my mooring lines; and there I floated snorting with astonishment and fear.

In the course of the day many other people

passed by, some lingering longer than others to step aboard without permission or have photos with one leg cocked on my bow. Children wagged my tiller back and forth. I thought it very dreadful, but the other boats moored beside me went on bobbing very quietly, and hardly raised their heads as the mucky-fingered, snap-happy things were ooo-ing and ahhh-ing over us.

For the first few days I could not float at peace; but as I found that this terrible creature never came into my cabin nor did me any harm, I began to disregard it; and very soon I cared as little for the pawing of a gongoozler as the other narrow boats did.

Since then I have seen many boats much alarmed and restive at the sight and sound of a canal enthusiast; but thanks to my good master's care, I am as fearless passing waterside beer gardens as on my own pontoon.

Now if any one wants to break in a new boat well, that is the way to do it.

My master once steered me as a pair with another narrow boat to the water point because it saved time filling our tanks simultaneously. She told me the better I behaved, the better I should be treated, and that it was wisest always to do my best to please my master. 'But', said she, 'there are a great many kinds of men: there are good thoughtful men like our master, that any narrow boat may be proud to serve; but there are bad, cruel men, who never ought to have a boat or a car to call their own. Besides these, there are a great many men foolish, vain, ignorant and careless, who never trouble themselves to think; these spoil more boats than any one, just for want of sense. They don't mean it, but they do it for all that. I hope you will fall into good hands; but a narrow boat never knows who may buy him, or who may cruise him. It is all a chance; but still I say, 'Do your best wherever you are, and keep up your good name.''

★ ★ ★

At this time I used to float by my pontoon, and my coat was polished every day till it shone like a rook's wing. Early in May there came a man from Squire Patrick's, who took me away to the Grand Union Canal. My master said, 'Goodbye, Darkie; be a good boat, and always do your best.' I could not say 'Goodbye', so I put my steel nose into his hand; he patted me kindly, and then I left my first home. As I lived some years with Squire Patrick, I may as well tell you something about the place.

Squire Patrick's mooring was very close to the Saltisford Arm, a short stretch of canal located in the town of Warwick. There was accommodation there for many permanent boats, on which families lived, as well as short-term visitors and two hire boats. As such, I was never lonely.

On the second day of my being there Squire Patrick took me out cruising. When we came home, his wife was on the towpath waiting as he tied up.

'Well Patrick, how does he go?'

'First-rate, love,' answered the squire. 'He is as fleet as a crippled deer, and has a fine spirit, too; but the lightest touch of the tiller will guide him. A pleasanter creature I never wish to captain. What shall we call him?'

'Would you like Ebony?' said she; 'He is as black as ebony.'

'No; not Ebony.'

'Will you call him Overdraught or Pound Eater or Aloan Again for the unjustifiably large sum you spent?'

'No; not any of those.'

'Then maybe Fishful Thinking or Aqua-holic or The Wet Dream?'

'No; he is too handsome to be strapped with a dumb play on words.'

'Yes,' she said, 'he is really quite a beauty, and he has such a throaty chug and such a paunched bow — what do you say to calling him Joseph after my father?'

'Joseph — why, yes, I think that is a very good name. If you like, it shall be so;' and that is how I got my name.

When Squire Patrick went to the pub later, he told his mates that his wife had chosen a good sensible English name for me that meant something; not like Blacked Beauty. They all laughed.

★ ★ ★

When the squire's wife died suddenly a few years later I was sold again. I was taken back to the Trent & Mersey Canal where I lived in a marina near Burton on Trent. It is a great thing to have a marina mooring. There are electric hook-ups and water points on every pontoon.

My new mistress patted me and spoke kindly. She said I would be turned into a bookshop but that she would keep my name because her favourite character of all the books she had ever read was called Joe. 'He is in a very famous horse story by a woman called Anna Sewell,' she said. 'He's introduced as the naïve stable boy who almost kills Black Beauty by not keeping him warm after his gallop to fetch the doctor. But Black

Beauty knows, for all his ignorance and faults, that Joe Green has a good heart. In the end, after Black Beauty has been passed from owner to owner, it is Joe who gets him because he has turned into the best and kindest of grooms.'

That spring, while she was working on fitting me out with her boyfriend and her parents, she read me the entire book from cover to cover. I cried when she got to the part where the horse is poorly and John, the coachman, is berating Joe's idiocy. 'Only ignorance! only ignorance,' he shouts, 'how can you talk about only ignorance? Don't you know that ignorance is the worst thing in the world, next to wickedness?' I often thought of John's words when I came to know more of the world, and when my mistress almost drowned me in a lock on the Leeds & Liverpool Canal.

* * *

I had many friends at the marina, among them a small green narrow boat called Apples. She was such a cheerful, plucky, good-tempered little boat that she was a favourite with everyone, and especially my mistress. Apples' owner lived far away in Australia but, when she visited, she always made much of me and would bring my mistress gifts too. They would chatter and laugh for hours together inside, drinking tea and planning trips out on us. I think I never saw my mistress so happy as when Amanda visited, for the marina, despite its shops and restaurants, was often a quiet place for her and she was lonely, even if she never admitted it to anyone.

There was another vessel that I became great friends with, and she was a wooden rowing boat called Josephine. My mistress painted her the same cream as my coachlines but I liked her best in the rust-red coat she arrived in, so I nicknamed her Ginger. Ginger had a bad habit of rocking her passengers almost into the water. One day she nearly tipped my mistress and her sister into the canal, and so after that my mistress was loath to take her out again. She still did some mornings, but they would leave early so no one could witness if they toppled. I don't think Ginger found pleasure in it. It was just a bad habit. She said no one was ever kind to her, and so why should she be steady. Of course it is a very bad habit; but I am sure, if all she says be true, she must have been very ill-used before she came here.

I was quite happy in my new place, and if there was one thing that I missed, it must not be thought I was discontented. All who had to do with me were good, and I had a spacious promenade mooring opposite a toyshop and a pub.

What more could I want? Why, liberty! For four years of my life I had had all the liberty I could wish for; but now, week after week, month after month, and no doubt year after year, I must be locked up except when I am wanted during business hours; and then I must be just as steady and quiet as any retail unit made of bricks and mortar. I must wear 'bookshop open' signs here and there, and have customers traipsing in and out and not buying anything.

Now, I am not complaining, for I know it must be so. I only mean to say that for a young boat, full of strength and spirits, who has been used to long canals where he can fling up his head, toss water from his propeller, gallop away at full 4mph speed, and then go round and back again with a 'toot toot' to his companions — I say it is hard never now to have a bit more liberty to do as he likes.

I think that after a year and a half my mistress realised this and maybe felt the same. Sometimes, tethered to the mooring rings, I have felt so full of life and spring that when Sarah has opened up shop in the morning I really could not keep quiet. Do what I would, it seemed as if I must bob, dance or prance; and many a good shake I know I must have given her, but she was always good and patient.

'Steady, steady, my boy,' she would say; 'wait a while, and we'll have a good swing, and soon get the tickle out of both our feet.'

★ ★ ★

I had often wondered how it was that my mistress was so very short of money; her income was really only enough to cover her outgoings and to buy in a few more books; and on one of our very quiet days in the marina I ventured to ask her by what accident she stayed so poor.

'Accident!' she snorted, with a fierce look, 'it is no accident! It is a cruel, shameful, cold-blooded act. When I was young, people used to buy their books in shops like ours. Now, however, they come in for ideas of new titles and to drink our free tea and then they buy them elsewhere.'

'How dreadful!' I exclaimed.

'Dreadful! Ah, it is dreadful! But it is not only the financial hit, though that is terrible and will last a long time; it is not only the indignity of having my hard work sourcing interesting titles and new authors taken from me for free, though that is bad; but it is this — how will any village or town or city bookshop ever be able to survive in future? People buy books without thinking of this, without considering what dull and draughty places their high streets would be without them. It's like Neil Gaiman wrote: 'A town isn't a town without a bookstore. It may call itself a town, but unless it's got a bookstore, it knows it's not fooling a soul.' I tell you it is a lifelong wrong, and a lifelong loss.'

'What do they do it for then?' said Ginger.

'For convenience!' said my mistress, with a stamp of her foot. 'For convenience! If you know what that means. There are few readers these days who do not prefer ordering a book from the comfort of their armchair in two or three clicks of the mouse to wandering into their local bookshop and taking time out to read staff reviews and diarise author events, or have the intent to buy just one book but, by the strange sorcery of those delicious places, come out with five instead, to meet like-minded people, to run their fingers down a hundred spines and feel, with every jolt of the track, the certainty that this journey is the most exciting one they will make for a long time.'

'I suppose it is convenience that makes

263

them use those horrid price checker apps or jot down ISBNs on a scrap of paper to order online later or to put in their trolleys at supermarkets,' said Ginger.

'Of course it is,' said Sarah. 'Convenience and cost-cutting and not enough appreciation for the value of books or the places that sell them. To my mind, convenience is one of the most wicked things in the world.'

My mistress, though she was gentle, was a fiery old thing; and what she said was all so new to me and so dreadful, that I found a bitter feeling towards men that I had never had before rise up in my mind. Of course, Ginger was much excited. With flashing eyes and a clap of her oars, she flung up her head, declaring that men were both brutes and blockheads.

'Who talks about blockheads?' said Apples, who just came back from refuelling. 'Who talks about blockheads? I believe that is a bad word.'

'Bad words were made for bad things,' said Ginger; and she told her what Sarah had said.

'It is all true,' said Apples sadly, 'but we won't talk about it here. You know the shop has regular customers, too, who are always good to it; and talking against men in such a place as this doesn't seem fair or grateful.

You know there are good book buyers elsewhere in the country too, though of course our regulars are the best.'

This wise speech of good little Apples, which we knew was quite true, cooled us all down, especially Sarah, who was dearly fond of her regulars; and to turn the subject I said, 'Can anyone tell me the use of Kindles?'

★ ★ ★

The longer I was used as a bookshop, the more proud and happy I felt at having all those stories and all that knowledge on sale inside me. One day, when Sarah had been out on some business at a school library, she came back much disturbed. At the school she had discovered a bloodied sanitary towel pressed between the pages of a reference book on cowboys. She told her friend Laura all about it, who laughed and said she had seen much worse at Cannock Public Library, where she once worked. Then she said how hard-hearted and horrible it was to wilfully damage books. But what stuck in my mind was this — she said that book vandalism was the devil's own trade mark, and if we saw any one who took pleasure in leaving menstrual paraphernalia between pages, we might know to whom he belonged, for the devil was a murderer from the beginning and a tormentor to the end. On the other hand, where we saw people who loved their books and were kind to hardback and soft cover, we might know that was God's mark; for 'God loves books.''

'You never said a truer thing,' said Sarah. 'People may talk as much as they like about their religion, but if it does not teach them to be good and kind to books and libraries and bookshops, it is all a sham — all a sham, Laura; and it won't stand when things come to be turned inside out and put down for what they are.'

* * *

One morning, early in May, Sarah started my engine and said now was the time to fight for what we believed in. She had brought food for a few weeks and a sleeping bag to lie in at night. We would be gone for six months, she told me. Then she started untying Ginger from my roof, who would make us too tall to fit under bridges. A new home had been found for her on the other side of the country. I held my face close to her, as that was all I could do to say goodbye; and then she was gone, and I have never seen her since.

My mistress's parents came to see her off and her father volunteered to come as far as Fradley Junction until she grew accustomed to handling me. He jumped aboard and we chugged slowly from my mooring and through the marina, where only a man called Ted was standing on his deck to have a last look and to say, 'God bless them!'

When we reached Fradley, Sarah's father jumped off and opened the last lock gate for us. I heard him say in his low gentle voice, 'Goodbye, Sarah; God bless you.' I felt her hand twitch on my tiller, but Sarah made no answer, perhaps she could not speak. As soon as he had driven away, Sarah went inside and stayed there a long time. Poor Sarah! She stood close up to my thin walls to hide her tears.

When it was gone mid-afternoon, Sarah came back out.

'We will not see these parts again for a very long time,' she said. She took the tiller, reversed me into a British Waterways working boat, and drove slowly away from home; but it was not our home now.

★ ★ ★

In Ginger's place my mistress saddled the length of my roof with green Astroturf. Some potted plants were also added. Now, when we were met by other boaters on the canal, they would call out nasty things about the way I looked. The vessels they captained were also rude. I have always suffered for my name, because it is a man's moniker in a very female environment. With pansies on my bow and a green plastic carpet on my back, boats insinuated I was effeminate and even the Mayor of Bath said I looked like a queen. Instead of looking forward with pleasure to passing other boats as I used to do, I began to dread it.

Sarah, too, seemed restless, though she said very little. She was attacked by canal purists for naming her business *The Book Barge*, where the correct term would have been *The Book Narrow Boat*, for my beam was less than seven feet. She bore it bravely and even consulted Samuel Johnson's 1755 *Dictionary of the English Language*, which reassured her the definition of a barge is: i) a boat for pleasure ii) a boat for burden. At last I thought the worst was over; for several days there had been no more taunts, and I determined to make the best of this trip and to do my duty, though now going out was a constant harass instead of a pleasure; but the worst was not come.

Hitherto I had always been driven by people who at least knew how to steer; but in Sarah's hands I was to get my experience of all the different kinds of bad and ignorant cruising to which we boats are subjected. It would take a long time to tell of all the different styles in which I was driven by her, but I will mention a few of them.

To begin with, she was a tight-tiller cruiser — someone who seemed to think that all depended on holding the tiller as hard as she could, never relaxing her hold or giving me the slightest liberty of movement. She was always talking about 'keeping the boat well in hand', and 'steering a straight course', just as if a boat would deliberately zigzag his way across the water.

After a few weeks of practice her confidence grew and she turned into a lazy cruiser, who let the tiller rest against her back while her hands were employed opening bottles of wine or reading a book. Of course, such captains have no control over a boat if anything happens suddenly. If a boat runs aground, or into low-hanging trees, or into a corner, they are nowhere, and cannot help the boat or themselves till the mischief is done.

Of course, for myself, I had no objection to it, as I was not in the habit of either pranging bridges or ploughing into banks, and had only been used to depend on my captain for guidance and encouragement; still, one likes to feel the tiller a little going around bends, and likes to know that one's captain has not gone to sleep.

Moreover, these captains are often altogether careless, and will attend to anything else rather than to their boats. I went out one day with Sarah and two of her friends. She flopped the tiller about as we started, and, of course, gave me several sharp thrusts of the throttle, though I was fairly off. We were cruising through London and there was a good deal of rubbish in the water. My mistress was laughing and joking with her friends, and talking about the buildings to the right and to the left; but she never thought it worthwhile to keep an eye on her boat, or to steer to the clearest parts of the canal; and so it easily happened that I got a traffic cone in my propeller.

Now, if any good captain had been there, he would have noticed that something was wrong before I had gone three paces. Even if it had been dark, a practised hand would have felt by my shuddering that there was something wrong, and would have put a hand down the weed hatch and picked out the obstruction. But this woman went on laughing and talking, while at every turn the cone became more firmly wedged between the blades of my propeller.

Whether my mistress was partly stupid or only very careless, I can't say; but she drove me with that cone in my prop for a good half-mile before she noticed anything was wrong. By that time I was going so slow that at last she paid attention, and called out, 'Well, here's a go! Why, we must be running out of diesel! What a shame!'

She then jerked the tiller and flipped about with the dipstick, saying, 'No, there's quite enough, so it's no use playing the old soldier with me; there's the journey to go, and it's no use turning lazy.'

Just at this time a young man came chugging near at the helm of a Camden trip boat; he lifted his hat and pulled up.

'I beg your pardon, miss,' he said, 'but I think there is something the matter with your boat; he goes very much as if he had something stuck in his propeller. If you will allow me, I will look down the weed hatch; these shopping trolleys and three-piece suites are very dangerous things for the boats.'

'He's a god-awful boat,' said my captain. 'I don't know what's the matter with him, but

271

it's a great shame to sell books from a crawling beast like this.'

The man came aboard, and, knotting his middle rope around mine, at once took a look at my prop.

'Bless me, there's a traffic cone. Crawling! I should think so!'

At first he tried to dislodge it with his hand, but as it was now very tightly wedged, he drew a penknife out of his pocket, and very carefully, and with some trouble, got it out. Then, holding it up, he said: 'There, that's the cone your boat has picked up; it is a wonder he did not stop turning altogether and ruin a blade into the bargain!'

'Well, to be sure!' said my mistress. 'That is a queer thing; I never knew before that boats picked up traffic cones.'

'Didn't you?' said the man rather contemptuously; 'but they do, though, and the best of them will do it, and can't help it sometimes on such canals as these. And if you don't want to ruin your boat, you must look sharp. This prop is very much bruised,' he said, setting the bar back across my weed hatch gently and patting me. 'If I may advise you, miss, you had better cruise him gently for a while.'

Then, boarding his own boat again, and raising his hat to the lady, he drove off.

When he was gone, my captain began to flop the tiller about and whip into full throttle, by which I understood that I was to go on, which of course I did, glad that the cone was gone, but still in a good deal of pain.

This was the sort of experience we narrow boats often had.

★   ★   ★

Then there was the steam-engine style of driving; this was mostly between towns when Sarah was always rushing to get ahead and open shop.

She always seemed to think that a boat was something like a steam engine, only smaller. And be the canals weed-ridden and shallow, or clear and deep, be they windy or straight, narrow or wide, it is all the same — on, on, on, one must go at the same pace, with no relief and no consideration.

This woman never thinks of getting up a little earlier to allow more travel time. Oh, no, she has pressed snooze on the alarm again, and rush she will! The boat? Oh, he's used to it! What were narrow boats made for, if not for speed? Leisurely chug! A good joke, indeed! And so the throttle is applied, and the tiller is jerked, and often a rough, scolding voice cries out, 'Go along, you lazy beast!' And then comes another kick of the throttle, when all the time I am doing my very best to get along, uncomplaining and obedient, though often sorely harassed and downhearted.

This steam-engine style of driving wears boats up faster than any other kind. I would far rather go twenty miles with a good, considerate captain than ten with my mistress; it would take less out of me.

Another thing — she scarcely ever equips me with fenders, however sorely I am scraped, and thus bad accidents sometimes happen; or if she does put them on, she often forgets to lift them up in locks; and more than once their ropes have snapped clean in half under the pressure they endure leaving its narrow walls; and that is a terrible strain on a boat.

Then this bookseller, instead of starting at an easy pace as a normal boater would do, generally sets off at full speed from the very lock gate; and when she wants to stop, she first leaps off, whips my ropes around a mooring bollard, and halts me so suddenly that I am nearly thrown over my nose, and my window is smashed from my frame when the metal hatch slams shut from it; she calls that pulling up with a dash! And when she turns a corner she does it as sharply as if there was no right side or wrong side of the canal.

★　★　★

I sometimes took as passenger a woman named Helena, who worked for a canalling magazine. She was a knowledgeable, competent captain, and had recently completed a helmsman course as a feature article for her publication. Still, there was an anxious look about her eye, by which I knew that she had some trouble with there being no toilet aboard. Like most of my mistress's visiting friends, I thought she had a very odd habit of crossing her legs, and then uncrossing them, and then making a little jump forward.

It was very unpleasant to watch for any boat who once boasted a toilet, and made me quite fidgety. When we got to midday, my mistress asked her what made her go in that odd, awkward way.

'Ah,' she said in a troubled manner, 'I know my bladder is very bad, but what can I do? It is really not my fault, it is just because I am desperate to wee. Although we have been away from a bathroom the same time today, your bladder is a good deal more practised than mine, and of course you can hold in much more, and go much longer. I wish I could have done so. All my present troubles come from my weak bladder,' said Helena, in a desponding tone.

Some girls, you know, are capital friends; but I think Sarah was a low sort of woman. She cared nothing now about basic human functions nor for finding a pub toilet for Helena to relieve herself; she only cared for going fast, but that would not do.

At the next lock she suggested Helena jump off and use the shrubs while we were waiting for the boat in front to pass through. Helena wandered off and Sarah busied herself with opening another bottle of wine. Just as she was pouring the first glass into a plastic beaker, we heard the lock keeper exclaim suddenly and start running towards the bushes, from which Helena flew in fright, still pulling up her knickers.

'That's my bloody garden you're pissing on,' he stormed, confronting the two girls, who were now holding hands and trembling violently on my stern. 'How dare you! What sort of creatures are you?' Poor Helena! I was very sorry for her, and I could not comfort her. I knew how hard it was upon Sarah's visitors to put up with her lack of facilities; and now this extra humiliation, and she can't help it.

Sarah pleaded very eloquently that her friend was rather admiring the topiary than doing anything so unwomanly behind the greenery. 'We are good, well brought up girls,' she kept repeating. 'Why should we ever do anything so awful as water your bedding plants from our lady bits?' To the girls' astonishment, the lock keeper accepted this defence, and even apologised for the accusation, which he now owned was rash and unfair.

The girls blushed and fell silent. My mistress took the tiller and they both turned from each other. I can remember now how quietly Sarah worked me through the lock, and then with a light hand and a gentle drawing of the throttle, we were off.

I arched my neck and set off at my best pace. I found I had someone behind me at last who was humbled and knew better how a good boat should be cruised. It seemed like old times again, and made me feel quite gay.

And so it came to pass that in the late summer Sarah finally found her way; and Helena even spoke to her again.

★ ★ ★

One morning, a few days after we had left Manchester, I was suddenly awakened by the alarm clock bell ringing very loudly. I heard the zip of Sarah's sleeping bag opened and her feet shuffling up the shop. Unusually, she was dressed in no time. She unlocked the front door and stepped onto the towpath, calling out, 'Wake up, Joseph, you must go well now, if you ever did!' and almost before I could think, she had slid my tiller on and started my engine. She just ran in for her coat, and then took me at a quick trot to the first lock.

'Now Joseph,' she said, 'chug for your life — that is, for your mistress's life; there is not a moment to lose.' She had promised use of the shop for a book club in Saltaire that night but had not thought to check quite how far away that place was first, nor to calculate how long it would take to cruise there.

After the lock there was a long piece of straight canal. Sarah said to me, 'Now, Joseph, do your best,' and so I did; I wanted neither throttle nor encouragement, and for many miles I cruised as fast as I could lay my hull to the water. I don't believe that any bookshop could have gone faster. When we came to a swing bridge Sarah pulled me up a little and patted my roof. 'Well done, Joseph! Good old fellow,' she said. She would have let me go more slowly, but my spirit was up and I was off again as fast as before.

The air was frosty, the sky bright, and it was very pleasant. We went through a village, through a dark wood, then downhill, then straight, till after ten hours we came just outside the place. On we went and into the last lock. All was quite still except for the clatter of my nose against the front gate. A clock struck three as Sarah began winding up the paddles.

I was glad to stop for a few minutes; my engine shook under me, and I could only bob and pant. It was then I noticed the gate was leaking. I soon had not a dry spot on my stern. The water ran down into the engine compartment too, and I steamed all over — Sarah later said, like a pot on the fire. Poor Sarah! She looked young and small up there above the lock, and she still knew very little; but I am sure she did the very best she knew.

When she saw, she tried pulling me out and she called for help, but she did not turn on my bilge pump. The knob to start it, in front of her all this time under the throttle, she believed was a hook for her handbag.

Soon I began to sputter and gasp, and the water turned deadly deeper; my engine submerged, and I felt scared all over. Oh! How I wished for the pump to churn it out as I started to slowly choke. I wished for her father or her old boyfriend to help, but they were over 100 miles away, so I lay down at the bottom of that lock and tried to go to sleep.

After a long while I heard Sarah at my ignition; I gave no sound as she kept trying the key, for I was too flooded. She was at my side in a moment, stooping down by me. I could not tell her how ill I felt; but she seemed to know it all. She braced her legs against the lock gate and pushed me partially out of the water's rush, then she ran up the ladder again to haul me out with the help of a man and two young children; then she tied me outside the lock and set to work with a plant pot bailing out water, which I was thankful for; then, I think, I went to sleep.

Sarah seemed very much put out. I heard her say to herself, over and over again, 'Stupid girl! Stupid girl! No idea where the bilge pump is, and I dare say the engine is finished now; I am no good.'

I was now very ill; water had come three-quarters of the way up my engine compartment, and I could not start without a fault alarm sounding and red lights flashing. Sarah bailed all afternoon. She would stand, water over her knees, scooping it out and back into the canal hour upon hour. A passer-by offered help, but she was too ashamed to accept it. 'My poor Joseph,' she sobbed to me, 'my good boat, you saved your mistress's life, Joseph! Yes, you saved her life.'

I was very glad to hear that. For so long I worried that she regretted buying me, and setting up shop, and losing money, home and her relationship, and leaving everything behind. I knew as much as this, that today Sarah said we must go at the top of our speed and that I had, for the sake of my mistress.

* * *

I do not know how long I was ill. The book club was postponed and I was left to rest and dry. Most days Sarah was quite silent but some nights, in the dark, I heard her say in a low voice:

'I wish, Joseph, you could say a bit of a kind word to me; I'm quite broken-hearted; I can't eat my meals and I can't smile. I know it was all my fault and, if you die, I will never forgive myself. I wish you might give me just a word.'

I heard no more of this soliloquy, for its medicine took effect and sent me to sleep, and in the morning I felt much better.

* * *

Sarah went on very well; she learned a little from this incident, and was so attentive and careful for the days after that I began to trust her in many things; but she had one great fault — the love of drink. She was not like some people, always at it; she used to keep steady for days or weeks together; but then she would break out and have a 'bout' of it, as I called it, and be a disgrace to herself, a terror to me, and a nuisance to all that had to do with her.

On the night of the postponed book club Sarah had some fifteen women aboard for it. They brought pizza and crisps, chocolate, and bottles of wine and spirits; and they set on these victuals with great enthusiasm. My mistress spoke in a very loud, off-hand way, and I thought it was very unlike her not to worry about red wine mixing with the pages of her books, as she was generally wonderfully particular about only drinking clear alcohol beside her stock. She came out neither at eight, nine, nor ten, and it was nearly eleven o'clock before she called me, and then it was with a loud, rough voice and to tell me she would be sleeping elsewhere that night. She seemed in a very good temper and laughed with one of the women, though I could not tell what over.

The woman's husband, come to take them

both home, stood at the hatch, and said, 'Have a care, Miss Henshaw!' but she answered sillily with a giggle; and almost before she was up my stairs she was staggering, frequently giving me a sharp cut with her elbow as she fell into me, though I was not rocking at all. The moon had not yet risen, and it was very dark. Having recently rained, my stern was slippery, and stumbling onto it like she did made her feet slide, so that she nearly skidded into the canal.

If Sarah had been in her right senses she would have been sensible of locking me up — and of something wrong with my ropes; but she was too madly drunk to notice anything. She soon recovered her feet and skipped to the road with her new friends, where she was driven to their home.

The moon had just risen above the hedge, and by its light I could make out my mooring lines lying undone a few yards beyond me. I did not move straight away. I could have groaned instead, for I was suffering intense pain both from my engine still and now the mess of upset wine and greasy crumbs inside me; but boats are used to bearing their pain in silence. I uttered no sound, but stood there and listened.

It must have been nearly midnight when I heard at a great distance the sound of more

283

inebriated footsteps. Sometimes the sound died away, then it grew clearer again and nearer. The road to Sarah's overnight lodging lay on the bridge in front of me; the sound came in that direction, and I hoped it might be her coming back to tie me up more securely and lock my hatch. As the sound came nearer and nearer, I was almost sure I could distinguish Sarah's step; but a little nearer still, and I could tell it wasn't her after all. I splashed frustratedly, and was terrified to hear an answering exclamation and men's voices. They came slowly over the bridge, and stopped in the middle to survey my swinging doors and slack ropes.

One of the men jumped down and jogged over to peer through my window. 'It is empty!' he said, 'and no one stirs.' The other man followed and bent over him. 'He's ours,' he said; 'see how the doors have been conveniently left open and the ropes near untied. Odd, though, that the boat has not moved from the place.' He then attempted to pull me closer to the bank. I made a step the other way, and he almost fell in.

Then followed a conversation between them, till it was agreed that Rob, the first to spy me, should lead me onwards, and that Kevin should board me and steer the tiller. I knew as well as they did what was going on and tried to stand still as stone.

Rob started off very slowly with his sad load, and Kevin leapt on the back and looked inside me and grabbed a half-finished bottle of Merlot from off the desk. And so they stole me. I shall never forget that night walk; it was almost a mile before they grew bored of the prank and went home to their beds. Rob had led me on very slowly, and I had limped and hobbled on as well as I could, suffering great worry. I am sure he was sorry for me, for he often patted and encouraged me, talking to me in a slurred voice.

Then they left me and I slowly drifted out into the middle of the water. Though the towpath now lay in the full moonlight, I could see no further motion. I could do nothing for myself. But, oh! How I listened for the sound of another boat, or wheels, or footsteps. The towpath was not much frequented, and at this time of the night I might stay for hours before help came to me.

I stood watching and listening. It was a calm, sweet October night; there were no sounds except a few low notes of a night-ingale; and nothing moved but the white clouds near the moon, and a brown owl that flitted over the hedge. It made me think of the autumn nights long ago, when I used to lie beside the duck Deirdre in the brown and pleasant canal of the Trent & Mersey. I waited, dreaming like this, for my mistress to find me again.

★ ★ ★

She came, in the end, late the next morning. Strange; I could not say that I remembered her, for she was grown more serious from the shock of seeing me gone, maybe wiser too, but I was sure that she knew me and that she had somehow changed in the short time, like that fictional stable hand Joe Green; so I was very glad. I put my nose up to her, and tried to say that we were friends. I never saw a woman so pleased.

PART THREE

50

TRENT (part i)

A quietness comes after Saltaire. I have stayed there for ten days in all, the longest the shop has been in one place since London. During that time it dried out. Then it floated away. I found it the next morning neatly filed on a long shelf of water between two mills, waiting.

And so we move on to Leeds. The weather too, which shakes us awake early each morning under a counterpane of frost. It has cold hands and the bad breath of damp leaves. My father visits. At 4 a.m. one morning I hear him reaching for the leftover bottle of Pinot to blanket his throat. The heating won't work until I fill up with diesel. The diesel won't be filled until I reach Leeds and sell some books. The cold makes my back tooth ache and I add 'dentist' to the growing list of swaps above my desk.

When I reach the city I moor in Granary Wharf, previously an old shopping centre built into the dark arches underneath Leeds railway station. It's a labyrinthine, dripping place, which has now been developed as a car park. However, the canal terminus has had a recent facelift and I enjoy the toilets of a shiny Mint Hotel and breakfasts at Out of the Woods café, both waterside and welcoming. A local band plays aboard and the whole weekend there is a pleasurable, mildly profitable one.

Before leaving I take the boat to Clarence Dock, Leeds' other big waterways development. It's home to the Royal Armouries Museum and I'm amused to find the military theme has extended to my canal boat neighbour for the night, who has converted his vessel into a German U-boat, of course. Painted battleship grey, with no windows, it has a conning tower, periscope and 'stealth hull'. I let out a squeal when I spy the captain himself, who is bearded and naval-uniformed and, I am slightly put out to realise, clearly far more ambitious with his boat than me. Where I have only typewriters and Babar the Elephant and Solzhenitsyn anthologies, he has sonar, whooper horn and Morse keys. For the first time in many weeks, I feel semi-grateful for the fake turf. 'Shove that up your imitation torpedo, Captain,' I mentally storm. Then a kid walks past with her parents and coos, 'Mummy, Daddy, LOOK! A funny-looking war boat,' and they all stand around taking pictures of it and don't so much as turn their heads when I stomp out with my big 'bookshop open' A-board and laminated 'author signing' posters. The good ship one-upman keels uncertainly beneath me.

All night the vision of Das Boot haunts my dreams. I'm annoyed at myself for getting so worked up about it. 'Joseph's a great boat,' I keep telling myself. 'He has bow thrusters and a literary canon aboard. Who needs to hunt destroyers when there is Proust to do battle with at bedtime reading? The bookseller's life is just as valid as the faux-submariner's,' I reason. But in the morning the U-narrow boat is the first thing I see when I open my doors: that impervious shell, the plastic arsenal. I want to challenge its captain to a barge pole joust but fear my blunt oak stump may be humiliated by a militaristically pimped bayonet fixing on his. So I chicken out and chug away, with just one final backward look at my nemesis. The boat seems to sneer after us. I bleed a little from the mouth, but it's only my dodgy tooth.

On the Aire and Calder Navigation en route to Keadby I look up and memorise German naval ranks. I start with petty officers and enlisted seamen but find the urgent harshness of the sounds so aligned with my dark mood that I soon move up the ranks all the way to Admiral. 'Oberleutnant zur See!' I bark delightedly at the power stations we roll past. 'Hauptgefreiter! Bootsmann! Oberstabsbootsmann! Flotillenadmiral!' I cry, throat to the grey sky and steam clouds. It makes a thrilling change from ordering jambon baguettes and, by the time I meet Stu later that evening to try our hand at navigating the River Trent, I'm high with confidence again and baying for adventure.

There's a great book by Sara Levine, another RL Stevenson devotee, called *Treasure Island!!!* (her exclamations). Loyal to the vigour of the original text, Levine's heroine determines to live by the sea adventurer's code of Boldness! Resolution! Independence! Horn-blowing! And so she sets out refurbishing her life with a parrot and P45, dumping her boyfriend, jilting her friends and chafing a good deal at the security of suburbia. I felt like this before I left home; I feel it again now I'm turning the boat's nose out of Keadby lock and back down the country once more. The lock keeper had suggested we might wait a day. There's a bore due tonight and bad weather on the way. The wave of water the tide will send down the Trent means we'll have to be out on it longer than usual, going all the way to Torksey because the current will be too strong to hold our mooring lines if we stop earlier, at Gainsborough. 'We'll be fine,' I assure him, Stu, and also two men on another narrow boat who are following behind us. 'We're on canal boats,' I add scornfully. 'What's the worst that can happen?'

For the first couple of hours I'm proved right. Stu has his feet up behind the tiller, a pair of my orange-rimmed sunglasses disarming the bright sunset he's steering into. I'm inside heating tomato soup on a camping stove and, in keeping with my new-found Germanophilia, trying to yodel the Lonely Goatherd song from *The Sound of Music*. For novices, we're both doing pretty well. Stu's following the map and avoiding the shallows, I'm already on verse three: 'A prince on the bridge of a castle moat heard / Lay ee odl lay ee odl lay hee hoo / Men on the road with a load of tote heard / Lay ee odl lay ee odl-oo / Men in the midst of a table d'hôte heard / Lay ee odl lay ee odl lay hee hoo / Men drinking beer with the foam afloat heard . . . SHIIIIIIIT!'

I run up the stairs with my pan of soup to see what Stu's cursing about. There's an enormous gravel barge bearing down on us and it's pretty frightening for a moment realising we have to cross in front to the wrong side of the river to give it the depth needed to pass us by. Afterwards we laugh it off though, and I take the tiller for a while so Stu can eat before the dark comes up properly. When it does, it brings rain. Soon after, lightning and thunder too. I take the map under the hatch lid and sit on the stairs, where it's drier, shouting up to Stu when islands or tight bends are coming so he knows which way to steer. We've turned off all the lights on the boat as the glare off the water was making it improbably harder to see. All we've left on is a red bike light Sellotaped on our port-side in case we meet another commercial vessel.

For some reason, the geography I see on the map isn't matching what Stu's getting outside. A couple of times I tell him to turn but there's no bend. Then, when one does come up unexpectedly, he pulls the tiller over too late, too violently, and the current swings us around in a 360 like a teacups amusement ride — on a log flume. It's terrifying and black except for the forks of lightning, and I start whimpering. I get the sole life jacket I have on the boat from the cupboard inside and present it to Stu. 'I think we're going to capsize. I want you to have this. I'm so sorry.' I look at him, mouth set in a grim line, eyes wide and still locked on the water in front. 'Get me the map,' he says, 'I can't figure out why we're not aware of these bends.'

I pass it over. The pages have thinned almost as much as my bravado in the storm. I can't quite believe the boat and the river are so out of our control. It's only 9 p.m. but the night looks much thicker than that around us. The wind is flying my hair at half-mast from under my hood and a recollection of the terrible history of that tradition flaps across my mind. It's seventeenth-century stuff — lowering a flag to allow 'the invisible flag of death' to fly atop. A way of signifying death's power, its presence. *But we're on canal boats!* I want to scream. *How can this happen?*

Suddenly, I'm all done with the lightning, and those little cutlasses of water slapping against my shop. I'm finished with the ripped roaring of thunder, the buccaneer currents that are taking my boat as their own. I sit down on the pooled stern and try, for the first time, to do something really brave. 'Stu,' I begin, but it's taken on the wind and slapped into a tree trunk on the bank so that he doesn't even register I've spoken. I get up again. 'Stu,' I say, this time right into his ear. He turns to me, and I'm surprised to find his mouth working at something too. He looks down at the map, his face twisted and confused. Is he thinking what I am? That there are other values than those espoused in kids' tales of classic adventure? That Boldness can be Love! That Resolution can be Empathy! That Independence can be Shared! That Horn-blowing could be learning the piano instead? He holds the map out to me. 'I'm lost without you Stu.' He doesn't hear because he's shouting louder. Above my words and the rain and that gale I can catch some of them: ' — ma — upside down! — idiot! YOU IDIOT!'

51

TRENT (part ii)

We miss the entrance to the mooring at Torksey, even with the map held correctly. We turn around and take a second go at it and then, finally tied up, find a pub. The other two men join us ten minutes later, similarly traumatised by the experience, and we all sit around filling out the horror from our cheeks with beer. I remember only two things about that bar. The first was that the lock keeper from Keadby walked in much later, and our new friends on the other narrow boat immediately jumped up, fists clenched, to seek retribution for sending us out on the river in such dangerous conditions. We hold them back and play down all the hazards, buy them more drink, find things to laugh about in the Trent's snapping water already. They take their stools again and content themselves with casting furious glances his way instead.

The other memory is of an old man with thick black hair, who sits alone at a table near us. He has been listening to our tales and comes over to chat. I can't help but stare at the well-carpeted scalp and rich noir shade and, seeing as I've survived the wrath of the Trent, figure his can't be nearly so bad and ask outright how he came to own such an alluring mop. The man is delighted I posed the question. 'Tug it,' he says, 'it's all mine, all natural.' I give it a firm pull and my companions do the same. We all nod respectfully at the truth of his words. The man tells us about a shampoo he has created to cure baldness. 'Look around you' — he waves a hand to the other drinkers — 'there's not a bare scalp among these boys. They all use it. It grows thick as wool.' I cast my eyes over all the men drinking to my left, whose manes are indeed black and thick. Then I shuffle around on my stool to survey the other half of the room, which is similarly hirsute. We are all incredulous. Just like that, the Trent curse is lifted. Our moods lighten. We get another round and discuss future voyages, Rapunzel tresses and all the bright things the voluminous future holds.

As Stu has work the next day my mum volunteers to drive over and take him back to his car, still parked near Keadby. By annoying coincidence the pub name we give her to find us is identical to another ten miles away, where she is waiting until last orders. When we do eventually meet, it's gone midnight and her purse has considerably lightened by crossing the toll bridge between the pubs four times in the confusion. After dropping Stu we get horribly lost again going through Gainsborough and it's 3 a.m. before we're back near the boat. 'Stay with me tonight?' I beg my mum, suddenly tired, childishly tearful, wanting her near. We walk down the long pontoon to the boat, the torch beam slipping between each plank into the rattling water below.

★ ★ ★

It was my mother who taught me to read. A lot of the time, growing up, it was the Bible. Our parents were church-going Christians and we attended a convent school run by an order of German nuns where scripture lessons were still part of the timetable. It's not a bad text to start with, not least because our mum had pledged a bowl of chocolate if we could recite the names of its sixty-six books from memory. We never succeeded and wreak Old Testament revenge on the empty Tupperware promise by taking turns to sit in it with our pants down when she was out of the kitchen and pull it from our cheeks with a fanfare of fart noise. Our giggles glittered that shiny kitchen floor.

In both *Oranges Are Not the Only Fruit* and her memoir *Why Be Happy When You Could be Normal*, the novelist Jeanette Winterson recounts her own, less happy, childhood with the Bible. Adopted by Pentecostal parents who expect her to grow up to become a missionary, she instead falls in love with a woman and is beaten, locked in a coal hole and exorcised. It is a tense, cold household of just six books. One is the Bible. Two others are commentaries on it. Winterson's own secret hoard of novels is discovered hidden under her mattress and burned on a pyre in the garden. She explains how, growing up, she needed the companionship and reassurance of words. Her mother hides a revolver in the drawer and longs loudly for the Apocalypse to come. She reads the Bible aloud for half an hour every night. Winterson remembers this in particular. Her mother's words have an arresting immediacy. No matter that they are centuries old, their power lingers.

During an assessment day for the primary school I was supposed to be following my siblings to, my mother was warned by the head teacher that I'd probably have to repeat the first year. In the five-and-a-half we've happily spent at home together baking cakes and 'fishing' the paper-clipped noses of cardboard trout with a magnet, it seems we've neglected my alphabet. I also failed the tying-a-shoelace test and am labelled with a 'balancing problem'. Hoping perhaps to kill *three* birds with one stone, my mother ordered a literacy programme called 'Stepping Stones' from the States and together we set out on the path to creating a phonetically skilled, more stable and securely shod little schoolchild before term started.

The initiative was slow to yield results. I resorted to employing my eldest sister, Clare, as scribe for my first valentine card. I was in love with my dark-eyed classmate Warren McGlone. 'Dear Worm,' she cruelly wrote, 'will you be mine?' I didn't understand his cold rejection until a friend pointed out the deliberate misspelling. He avoided me for the rest of the month. Jeanette was right — the words carry on doing their work. I vowed to learn them all.

⋆　⋆　⋆

That night my mother and I sleep side by side, on the floor, for the first time since those years. We are cradled by a black boat that doubles as a bookshop. There are so many words shelved above us and behind us but only two, joined at the hip, that we smile across the shared pillow.

'Night-night.'

'Night-night.'

I sleep better than I have in many months. In the morning, early, she stands on the pontoon, one hand on her hip, the other waving me off. It could be my first day of school. It could be the moment I've loved her most.

52

TRENT (part iii)

I'm bound for Newark. It is a fine morning, the river laid out like a hopscotch grid to skip over. On the bank a drag hunt canters along with us for a while. The riders slow and raise their hats and I whoop and wave crazily back.

The pattern of water and field and sky is an easy one to follow. There are hardly any buildings hemming the sides and a curious freedom fills up from my feet. These are the moments I own. When people ask, 'What did the months give you?' I can open a wardrobe dressed with them. Yes, I would show how each day has been altered somehow. Let out a bit here to catch the wind, pressed and pleated where I have sat too long on the rail over the stern kicking my feet to headphone pop and the low bass of the engine. Look at the darts sewn in: here where a great bird of prey tucked his wings on my bow, here where two kids jumped on and begged we race their dad on the towpath. They added form, they made a better fit. These months have been a good tailor. They sized me well.

So I laugh, peeling off the life jacket and hoods and waterproof trousers and Morrisons bag socks, when I see the expression on Graeme's face in Newark. *This is a new low*, he gestures. He sees the mud and the unwashed hair and the pyjamas peeking over my boots. I give a twirl. We go out for lunch and I tell him how wonderful it would be to fill the hull with water and have a swimming pool inside; to be able to float down the Trent on a Lilo on a boat, looking up at the ambling sky.

In Nottingham — my last call before home — there are few customers. I spend the weekend increasingly anxious about going home. I clean a lot, which is weird for me. I grow very quiet. On the Sunday afternoon, attempting a detailed commemorative brass rubbing of the last pound coin in my till, my nerves are wracked further by an enormous crash on the roof. I race outside to see a man prostrate on its green turf, having flung himself from the bridge above. Although the novelty of having someone risk life and limb to come aboard can't be underestimated, I quickly realise he's a) fine b) drunk and c) the star of a sick mobile phone stunt, which is being filmed by three mates still on the bridge. That gets me yelling and, because I'm moored next to the city courts, brings a couple of policemen over, one of whom gives chase down the tow-path. The other comes inside for a cuppa and to enlighten me on Nottingham's violent crime figures, which causes an ugly accident with hot tea and an ill-timed snort of panic over my unfinished rubbing.

Of course, it's not all bad. For a start, Nottingham boasts the only pub in the UK where the canal runs inside the building. It immediately pisses all over the Vietnamese floating bar experience I paid a small arm and a leg for on a south-east Asian tour — previously my only other aquatic drinking establishment experience. We were taken out of sight of the coast on a small motor boat, thrown off with a rubber ring stringed with local lager, and told through a megaphone at regular intervals to 'Party! Party HARD!' until my fingers went blue from the cold and my chattering teeth cut splinters of glass from the green bottle neck of my Bia Saigon.

It's just outside Nottingham that I also spy something I've been looking for the entire time I've been on the canals: a boat with my name on it. The Sarah Louise is as black as Joseph and almost as long. I pull over, take a couple of pictures of the pair of them, and chug away down the Trent & Mersey a whole lot more satisfied than when I left it.

The last evening I spend on the boat is Halloween. The clocks have already gone back and so, by the time I've moored and swept leaves off the roof, it is a dark walk to the nearby village where tea-lighted pumpkins and cardboard skeletons glower from doorsteps and windows. I meet some friends for dinner and after, back in the shop by myself, I cut a crescent moon with a teaspoon into the latest customer-baked Victoria sponge. It is soul cake, I think — the small round cake traditionally made for All Saints Day or All Souls' Day in memory of the dead. It's a pastime that preceded — and perhaps inspired — the trick or treating that's become customary today. On Halloween they were given to small children and the poor (collectively called 'soulers') as they traipsed from door to door singing and saying prayers for the deceased. People gave the cakes to symbolise souls being released from Purgatory.

I think of all the cakes I've collected on this trip, which were perhaps given in a similar vein. I've chugged from town to town, eulogising a dying breed of shop, desperately trying to prolong the life of my own. It's been a kind of purgatory maybe, that temporal state of punishment and purification; the waiting period to find out your fate. We learnt a psalm at that convent school about it, Psalm 66. 'We went through fire and through water,' it said. And all the while the indulgences of customers with their credit cards, the kind prayers of bloggers and the Twitterverse. And those cakes again. Those mountains of cake. The soul of the jammy sponge.

'Nice idea, Sarah,' I say aloud in the candlelight. 'Call it a purgatory but you're not fooling anyone. It's a convenient word to sweep away the good ol' Catholic guilt of consuming an unholy amount of calories.'

53

HOME

The Book Barge arrived back at Barton Marina on 1st November 2011. Six months had passed since it set out from there that bright morning of early May. It had chugged some 1,079 miles through 707 locks, sold 1,172 books and bartered 223. I was never much of one for numbers but, for a while, I liked the look of these ones. A photographer for a local newspaper made me spell out 1,000 miles in books on the promenade and pose sitting on the bow of the boat looking uncomfortably across at them. After that I didn't much fancy them any more but I found, when I went to write a blog about being back, I had no words to replace them with.

I had two days off before I opened the shop again. I spent most of these in front of the laptop trying to work out a way to explain how I felt, with only these numbers and no words of my own. In the end I borrowed some, and they served very well. They were from *The Wind in the Willows*, Chapter Seven, which is called The Piper at the Gates of Dawn. It's a long chapter, a slow, meditative one. People often forget it's in the book as it jars against the sandwiching tales of Toad and Badger and, later, the wicked weasels and stoats. Some abridgements and dramatisations leave it out altogether. It describes Mole and Rat's search for their friends the otters' missing son — a successful one, it turns out. On the way home there's an exchange which I think better sums up experiences on the waterways than their other, much more celebrated one, about the pleasures of messing around in boats:

'I feel strangely tired, Rat,' said the Mole, leaning wearily over his oars, as the boat drifted. 'It's being up all night, you'll say, perhaps; but that's nothing. We do as much half the nights of the week, at this time of year. No; I feel as if I had been through something very exciting and rather terrible, and it was just over; and yet nothing particular has happened.'

So I went back to the boat and opened up and, after a week, there was the horrible realisation that the cycle could repeat itself; that business would slowly slump again, that debts would need repaying increasingly urgently, that the question of closing would rear its ugly-looking head again. And I was right about the first two. Strange, though, that this time I never considered the latter.

54

PARIS (part i)

This is how it should end: on the Canal Saint-Martin in Paris, late November. And here I am, standing on one of its iron bridges. Every so often the dry leaves all flap up from the towpath at once and, because I am crying, I feel caught up in the snow globe of their winter patter. I have a round, brown shoulder bag, a laptop in a rucksack and a black suitcase on wheels. I carry exactly one month's worth of clothes, spread between the three bags, and my children's city map, which places me on the Passerelle Bichat, not far from a park called the Jardin Villemin.

From this vantage point I can look across, over the lock, to its iron gate opposite — the exact same one Audrey Tautou stands on, red-frocked, to skip stones on the water in the film *Amélie*. I have carefully imagined this moment many times. I know every detail of how the canal sits like a broken elbow in a grey cast of roads. I know which books reference it and just how The Book Barge will lie here one day, green-lit by spring. I know how, on the set of *Amélie*, they resorted to CGI for the stone skipping because Audrey Tautou couldn't do it right. Yes, it is all a trick.

I come to Paris looking for a glorious end. The boat has been back just a fortnight. My customers say, 'You went. We assumed you had closed.' I ball up my fists while they ask: 'But what will you do now?' I run again. I come to Paris with £100 and a month's worth of clothes in a round, brown shoulder bag, a rucksack, and a black suitcase that lost a wheel at St Pancras. I pull it from the station to the Seine, down to the cobbled walkway and up to Shakespeare & Company, the famous bookshop, where I ask to sleep in return for free labour. They have no room. I never thought of that. I walk the entire length of the canal and back down to this bridge. The suitcase follows, tottering on that single foot.

There is no plan now. I was to research and secure a mooring, learn French, make money, come home for Christmas and back with the boat in spring. Here, now, I can do nothing but stand on a bridge and cry. It feels too difficult. I came with a deep coat pocket of pebbles to bounce on the water. I see every one splash once and sink. I see them grow to huge Sisyphean boulders on the canal bed. I am suddenly tired of the useless efforts and unending frustration.

That night I sleep in a hostel dorm and early the next morning I walk back to the train station and go home.

★ ★ ★

Laura says, 'Did you ever discover who was text-stalking you on the boat all those times?' I shake my head and show her the latest messages, because they haven't stopped. She's fuming. 'And you still have no idea who he is?' I shake my head. 'Well then it's time to find out.'

She copies the number from my screen and presses 'call'. After ringing for a minute or so it's diverted to voicemail, so Laura leaves a garbled message saying: 'I'm in the pub waiting for you still. I've been here two hours now. I'm getting really worried that you haven't showed up. Call me in the next five minutes or I'm calling the police to report a missing person.'

We sit back and sip our wines. Sure enough, before five minutes is up her phone beeps and it's a text from him: 'You have the wrong number.'

Laura persists: 'I'm so sorry. I must have slipped to the wrong person in my contacts list but for some reason your name isn't showing. Who is this? I'll re-save.'

Reply: I'm Taj Wong. From Barnet. Who are you?

Laura: That's a name you don't forget in a hurry. But I have ... Is your pic on Facebook?

Reply: Yes, let's be friends.

We pore over his profile. I've never seen him before, I'm sure.

Laura texts: You look familiar. Did we meet on The Book Barge maybe? Are you friends with the owner?

Reply: The Boat (sic) Barge? I went on once earlier in the summer. I never talked to her though.

Mystery solved. We clink glasses. He is a nutter, yes, but not one I'm likely to bump into again. We pretend to hit typewriter keys and hum the *Murder, She Wrote* theme tune. Laura's phone beeps again.

Weirdo: Hey, I can tell without even looking on your Facebook picture that you're hot, Laura.

Later: You sound really sexy in your texts. Want to meet up?

Several texts even later: Laura? Are you still there? Call me?

Laura says, 'What must be going on in his head? How estranged from reality must he be to put his shit out there, sit back, and expect a happy ever after to come boomeranging straight back to his inbox. He's delusional!'

But he kept doing it. Now he would send the same message to both of us. We would ring each other when we received one, continually amazed at his brazenness and stupidity and tenacity and downright cheek. I saw his boulder rolling up in 140 characters, and straight back down when we pressed delete. And again the next day. And again the day after. Albert Camus, in his 1942 essay *The Myth of Sisyphus*, found the ceaseless struggle an apt metaphor for the absurdity of human life. But he saw something else in it too. 'One must imagine Sisyphus happy,' he said. 'The struggle itself towards the heights is enough to fill a man's heart.' So I thought: I'll roll up my sleeves with the worst of them. I'll do as Taj Wong. I'll do as I've been doing. I'll keep opening shop, and I'll keep up the dream, and I'll probably keep getting into more debt.

55

PARIS (part ii)

I don't know how actual cities can hear a person's thoughts but Paris somehow got wind of this foolish plan of mine and went: 'Jeez, really? You're just going to carry on making the same mistakes? Are you *completely* nuts?' But obviously Paris said this in French, and too fast, so I didn't quite catch what she meant even when I asked, really politely, 'Repétez s'il vous plaît?' So Paris called me back to see her just a month later. This time, she didn't use anything nearly so subtle as sinking pebbles and no room at the bookshop and broken suitcase wheels to tell me to sort my shit out. She used a dead bookseller instead.

George Whitman is the reason I came into bookselling. He owned the famous Paris bookstore Shakespeare & Company, which, as all bibliophiles know well, sits on the banks of the Seine in the shade of Notre Dame and literary legend. It was here in Whitman's 'rag-and-bone shop of the heart' that Samuel Beckett and Henry Miller, Lawrence Durrell

315

and William Burroughs, Jack Kerouac, Allen Ginsberg and Arthur Miller, and countless other great writers and complete novices too could pop by and browse books, borrow them, buy them, talk, write, sleep and feel at home. It was managed with financial carelessness and great eccentricity. There was a dictum of kindness to strangers and a mysterious back story that started in America and took in the Panama jungles and mangrove swamps before arriving in post-war Paris — specifically, in a modest lending library operating from a hotel bedroom. I wanted to be George. Or at least to marry him.

When he died, aged ninety-eight, on 14th December 2011, I sent an email to his shop. It didn't say much; nothing more than what I just told you — that George Whitman was the reason I came into bookselling. And that was that. Except a few days later I got sent funeral details, probably by accident. This time I didn't have money for the train over so I rang my brother: 'We don't see so much of each other these days,' I began. 'What we need is a day trip. (Paris? You drive? Hang out at a funeral?).' And, because Paul is Paul, he paused only half a beat before saying: 'Sure.' And then, after some more thought: 'Will there be loads of cool people there and will I have to wear some black clothes that are also cool clothes?'

When we get to the Père Lachaise cemetery there's some confusion with the car because of my bad language skills. The gatekeeper is led to understand we're part of the cortege and ushers us through into the graveyard itself, where we can't find a regular place to park so have to dump it behind some pretty big mausoleums. We feel bad about this — and worse when we see that all the cool young people wearing cool black clothes by the main building are clutching single roses, while we come bearing no bouquet. Paul says, in all seriousness: 'At least I got dressed up.' He is wearing an all-black Superdry shell suit and holding a matching black Superdry laptop bag. After a while, someone approaches us and says something in French, which is probably: 'How did you know the deceased?' Or: 'Where is your rose?' Probably the latter, in fact, because a couple of minutes later a woman takes pity on us and volunteers her own flower for me to hold instead. We follow the funeral party down the stairs to a chapel (a little earlier than I had been told it started), and pile in with the other mourners. There's a chance to view the body but the press of people doesn't permit this. We stand, respectfully, somewhere in the middle of the throng and wait for the service to begin.

Now the weird thing is that although George Whitman was American, they've chosen to conduct the service in French. I try really hard to follow proceedings but after a while I kind of zone out and start studying the faces of the people around us. The first thing I'm surprised at is how upset people are. I don't mean that callously — despite not having been to many, I do realise it's a standard feature of most funerals to weep a little and be sad. No, what startles me is that the scale of mourning is tipping to the hysterical and uncontrolled which, considering George was ninety-eight when he passed, I maybe wasn't expecting so much. The mourners are also very young; hardly more than teenagers. We're in a room of very young, very upset students and that's when I, at least, begin to feel a little bit anxious. I try to pay more attention to the speaker to take my mind off the woman to my right, who is loudly inconsolable. The speaker is telling a long story about the deceased but what keeps coming through, even with my limited French, is that the deceased was a beloved friend, a beloved son and a beloved grandson. He says it again: There couldn't, in fact, be a better friend or a better son or a better grandson. The last words make me sway. The woman next to me gives a sympathetic smile and sniff. I tug at Paul's arm until he looks over. 'He was ninety-eight,' I mouth.

'Thanks for the translation,' Paul whispers back sarcastically.

'Noooo, no no,' my mouth goes. 'He was ninety-eight! Who in this world is still a grandson at ninety-eight?' And that's when we both pale and learn how terrible a thing it is to drive all the way to Paris and attend the wrong stranger's funeral.

I put a tissue over my face, ostensibly to hide my grief. More usefully, it masks my shame. We grab each other's hands, put our heads down, and push as politely but as hurriedly as we can through all the sobbing people to the exit. Outside, we cannot speak. We only bite our lips and shake our heads and wring our hands.

Despite all this we find George's funeral before it has even begun. Sitting meekly at the back, we look at our feet and at the black-and-white photograph on the order of service. George stares out, looking beyond us; a thumb buttoning his mouth, two fingers resting a cigarette. His hair, which he trimmed by singeing the ends with a candle, hangs cursive over his forehead.

When we leave a man is handing out copies of George's three favourite books. One is

Don Quixote, one is a Walt Whitman anthology. But the one pressed into my hand is Dostoevsky's *The Idiot*. My brother and I look hard at it. We remember the lines of the poem read out in the service: *Camerado, this is no book.*

> *It is I you hold and who holds you,*
> *I spring from the pages into your arms*
> *— decease calls me forth . . .*

It is a symbol, a *message*. It may have taken a while but here, on the white steps of Père Lachaise, I finally get it loud and clear. And so it was written: The Idiot, the idiot, the *idiot*. And so I am.

> *Dear friend whoever you are take this kiss,*
> *I give it especially to you, do not forget me,*
> *I feel like one who has done work for the day to retire awhile . . .*

56

PLAN

After my appraisal, George rests in peace while I go home to consider all the ways I have been an ass. Mostly I do this by staring out of the porthole window at the marina, at the dual carriageway and the Argos warehouse but, on one morning, my gaze is instead drawn to a half-submerged cruiser on the pontoon opposite. It is Ted's boat.

It's unclear whether he died before the boat sank (his breathing had been worsening in recent weeks) or whether, when the boat went down in the night, he did with it. Afterwards, though, it comes to light that Ted's boat had been sinking for a very long time. He had been bailing out water from a small leak for months with a bucket. When I hear about this it doesn't surprise me but rather comes with a jolt of recognition: I think, 'So *he* was a stubborn fool, too.' We had more in common than I ever allowed. Because watching the efforts to lift his boat out of the water is too horrible, I move away from the window to my desk. I turn the clock that only ticks on its back onto its back, count twenty beats and then empty every drawer of the filing cabinet onto the floor. Bank letters, book invoices, court threats, overdue notes; their white envelopes pool into so many overlapping fault lines. Not bothering to clear a space, I sit down on the fragile tectonics of my arrears.

★ ★ ★

A friend of a friend asks what my exit strategy is. 'Eh?' I say. We are sitting eating dinner and I hope that by tactically knocking over my glass of water I can avoid further questioning. He follows me into the kitchen where I'm opening cupboards looking for paper roll to dry off my placemat and skirt. 'You've had fun, it's been an 'experience' . . . ' I cut him off before he's finished squatting his index fingers up and down around that horrid word.

'In fact, I'm drawing up a plan this very evening,' I smile brightly. 'A five-point plan. A model of good business-ness.'

He nods sympathetically and puts a hand on my shoulder. 'That's sensible. I'm pleased you've come to the same conclusion as all of us.' He waves towards the dining room with his other arm. I follow the direction of his gesture to the small group around the table who are laughing together over a video on someone's phone.

'Actually I'm not sure exit plan is quite the right word . . . '

'What would you call it then?' he asks, his hand moving across to my far shoulder and drawing me in for an awkward side-hug.

'A 'departure', certainly, from how I've been running things before — but it'll still essentially be a mostly unprofitable floating bookselling enterprise.'

His hand loosens.

'Maybe 're-entry' is a better description,' I continue. 'A five-point plan for magnificent re-entry. Hey, we could meet up sometime to discuss it. Just, y'know, to make sure we're on the 'same page'.' I air-quote like he did before quietly joining the others

★　★　★

The first step is **buying a shredder.** I pick out a really cute, healthy-gummed, brown-and-white baby rabbit for the task and train him up quickly on a couple of small jobs; a mooring fees reminder and a national insurance contribution statement. He's a fast worker so I prolong my enjoyment by feeding the next few through an old Underwood typewriter. He stands on his back legs, front paws scrabbling for qwerty and, after a false start with the ink ribbon, sets on the bounced direct debits with relish. I start to like this animal a lot. I call him Napoleon Bunny-parte, which I sincerely hope won't give him a complex.

Obviously, destroying the evidence doesn't undo the financial crime. My wholesale accounts are suspended until I pay what's owed. My cards are also stopped, both personal and business ones. I need to **get cash quick** and, as often happens to the financially wretched among us, I find myself in the office of a payday loans company. Except, rather than borrowing money, I'm proposing they just give it to me. Give me rather a lot in fact because I'm negotiating they hire me as a writer. I've read the shitty letters these firms send out — lots of them. And I know for a fact that most recipients take just one glance before serving them up with a carrot top and carriage return lever to their pet bun. I get a trial period and prove rather adept. I extend my letter-writing reach with some other freelance work communicating the importance of having comprehensive income protection insurance. *Have you ever thought how you'd pay that pile of bills without a regular salary?*

Twelve months later, with my money

replenished, creditors appeased and my notice handed in, it's time to move on to the next stage of the grand plan, which is how to make the bookshop financially viable long-term. I've gleaned two buzz words in the year of corporate whoring that I'm not afraid to whip out again for the punters: diversify and educate. The latter strikes me as relatively obvious. Go into schools in a guise of semi-authority (librarian, horn-rimmed glasses, pencil skirts) and use every means at your disposal to get kids hooked on books. Stick up 'Champions Read!' posters! Dabble in DVD adaptations! Lure them in with Harry Styles stickers! Then fill their open arms with vampire schmaltz and zombie apocalypses and lashings of free bookmarks, nigh blowing the entire library budget in a fortnight and directing them to their nearest and dearest local floating retailer for their next reading fix.

I was less confident with the 'diversify' brief. I've tried many things in the past, from conkers on pretty string (both page marking AND autumn gaming potential) to late night 'shopping by tealight' on Halloween (wax-damage to stock; not enough illumination to administer the correct change). 'Buy one, get one RRP' stickers, hand-knitted book warmers and a self-published *Bake Your Own Royal Wedding* cookbook have also failed to give any significant boost to takings. After churning the idea over for several months, I figure the best I can do is retro-fit a toilet to encourage longer browsing.

This takes me up to point five of the five-point plan: **the wildcard.**

57

WILDCARD

I write to Jeff Bezos, founder, president and CEO of amazon.com. Actually, I don't. I write to a small business in Australia called Clothing for Correspondence which, as the name suggests, satisfies all a client's communication needs in return for items from their wardrobe. A devotee of the good swap to the end, I send them my brief with a green belt and fetching scarf/glove set. Here's what I receive back:

Dear Jeff Bezos, founder, president and CEO of amazon.com,

Are you a fan of Meg Ryan? It's okay if you're not. She sells a certain type of cute that's not everyone's cup of tea. What about romantic comedies in general? I'm not talking Aniston or Heigl, god help us all, I'm talking the classics, like The Shop Around The Corner. *It's a 1940s film that sees two warring shop assistants 'unexpectedly' fall in love with each other as anonymous pen* pals. Whacky, huh? Your local video shop will probably have it.

In 1998 a remake of dubious quality was made, called You've Got Mail. Meg Ryan plays Kathleen Kelly, owner of *The Shop Around the Corner*, a charming little bookstore crammed with quirks and family values. Tom Hanks plays Joe Fox, top shot executive of Fox & Sons, a nasty big chain bookstore, which threatens to obliterate Kathleen's livelihood. Little do they know, they're corresponding anonymously via the deliciously modern media of 'the chat room' and 'electronic mail' and, you guessed it, falling in love.

Things have changed since 1998. Firstly, it's no longer possible to fall in love anonymously over the internet. If Kathleen Kelly could have Googled NY152, emailer-of-her-dreams, she would have traced him back to Joe Fox, executor of her business nightmares. Their little love affair would have come to a screeching halt.

Secondly, fear of the department-style bookstore now seems amusing and old fashioned. All because you, Jeff Bezos, were ahead of the game. As early as 1994 you were founding amazon.com, a little idea that would have made both Kathleen Kelly and Joe Fox shudder with dread. 'Selling books in a store?' you were laughing. 'Quit flirting in chat rooms, kids, and start using those boxy laptops for your own capitalistic gain!'

Are we both thinking the same thing, Jeff Bezos? Given how things have changed in the book business since You've Got Mail, and given your leading role in this change, perhaps it's time for a remake! In our new version, you will star as you — founder, president and CEO of amazon.com — and I will star as me. In the interest of modernisation let's drop the antiquated theme of anonymity. My name is Sarah Henshaw. I live in the UK and run a small independent bookshop on a converted narrow boat called The Book Barge. You can find me on Twitter, Facebook and my blog.

Full confession: my heart didn't exactly skip a beat when I saw your pic on Wikipedia. That said, when I read you made Forbes' Billionaires list, I fancy I did feel a little flutter. In the interest of this being a romantic comedy, I'm willing to kiss you at the end.

Full confession, part two: there's a twist in this new version. I joined the bookselling business already knowing of your reach. I joined because I knew independent booksellers were being put out of business and I wasn't happy about it.

I'm not hapless like Kathleen Kelly, who closes The Shop Around the Corner and trades in bookselling for a career as a children's author. I'm going to continue selling books because I believe there's room for us both. I'm not completely without entrepreneurial understanding; I get where you're coming from with amazon.com. Warehouses offer far better book storage than a narrow boat, book storage increases choice and customers love choice. Warehouses also allow for bulk purchasing which leads to cheap books and customers love cheap books.

What I'm scripting for our film is that you start to understand where I'm coming from. You climb on board my narrow boat (not a euphemism; this film is PG) and discover that book-selling can be an art. And because wealthy people love art, you're insatiably intrigued. You invite me out to dinner, somewhere with tablecloths and candlelight and Beethoven's Moonlight Sonata playing in the background. Over oysters and champagne, you ask me if it's hard running a business day-in day-out, while knowing the financial return will hardly cover the bare necessities of food and shelter. I say, 'Sure, it's hard. But satisfying too.' My eyes light up as I explain how passionate I am about selling books and bringing a book-shop to the people via the canals, from no fixed address. You say, 'It's kind of like selling books on the internet, then?' I say, 'Kind of, but not.'

Then I explain how it's not only a space to buy books but also to attend readings and meet fellow booklovers and writers and like-minded souls. I tell you how thrilled people are when they discover The Book Barge. How it taps into something romantic that's in all of us.

At the mention of romance, members of the audience who are experienced viewers of romantic comedy will think 'here we go!' and lean a little forward in their seats.

But we defy their expectations and our conversation turns instead to the topic of wealthy benefactors. I tell you about how, in the olden days, benefactors were all the rage. How it was an integral form of philan-thropy to show support and appreciation to those who were pursuing non-lucrative, yet culturally and creatively valuable careers. I tell you that, without his wealthy benefac-tor, we wouldn't be sitting here listening to Beethoven's Moonlight Sonata.

Spoiler alert: by the end of this film, you and I will have single-handedly resurrected the patronage system. As promised, there's a kiss. It's not a 'promise-of-things-to-come' kiss. It's more of a 'Thank god you're not putting me out of business or taking over The Book Barge' kind of kiss. The kind of kiss that says loud and clear, 'Thank you for appreciating the art in what I'm doing and providing me with no-strings-attached financial backing.'

You know the kind, right? Give me a call to find out more . . .

Yours sincerely,

Sarah xxx

58

STUPID

I've got mail — but not from Jeff. I recognise the handwriting as Stu's; the 'I's left undotted, the slight lean of the lettering. The white envelope is made up of two smaller ones cut along their bottoms and slid together. A single wrap of clear Sellotape holds them in place and bisects the final envelope. If it were not for this tape and the blue-inked address, the envelope would be the same as any number I used to receive when I owed all that money. The stamp has an orange London 2012 Olympic logo on. Nothing about this envelope makes me want to open it. It just makes me feel sick.

Since that moment on the Trent, I've not made any more attempts to tell Stu how I feel. We continued seeing a lot of each other for a while after I got home, but a strange tension slowly built. Perhaps he, too, expected me to give up on the bookshop now. I remember a conversation we had around that time about what we would spend our fortunes on if either of us won the lottery. Stu said he'd pay for a big crane to take the boat out of the water and squash it to the size of a steel Lego brick.

He used to pop by the shop on his way home from work. There he'd find me, feet haloed by fan heaters, the kettle button pressed down with a dictionary to keep a steady breath of steam on my cold cheeks. He would wait at the back, by the poetry and new releases and biscuit tin, until I'd finished with whichever customer was asking about the free tea or if my books got particularly damp being on a boat. I'd have to explain that the humidity had more to do with the Morphy Richards geyser I'd created on my desk and, besides, that I was partial to a bit of condensation on my windows for all sorts of reasons. When they left, he'd wordlessly get the 'bookshop open' sign in from outside and bring the tiller in for me overnight too. He'd give the rabbit a friendly nose-rub and wait for me to cash up. Sometimes he'd be waiting a long time because there simply were no takings to count and this used to make us bicker.

★   ★   ★

When I met Stu it was very different because we didn't use to talk, let alone argue. We worked together — me behind the bar, he as duty officer — at a local sports centre. He would come then, as he did on the boat, to take the till reading at the end of the night and check the float. When I heard the bar door open and then the ring of the cash register, I would walk straight out the kitchen door behind it and along the corridor to the cleaning cupboard. Sometimes I would nip into the ladies toilet first to check my hair. Then I'd head back to the bar, dragging the big Hoover they had there and, so he would never know I was in love with him from my clumsy answers or dry mouth, I'd make sure I was vacuuming the entire time it took him to fill in his sheets and check I'd restocked the fridges. Inside the cloud of noise and bustle I created, I was always floating just being in the same room as him.

We'd perhaps only exchanged seven words to each other when I received a text really late one night a couple of months later. It just said: 'Been thinking about this for a while, but do you want to go for a drink sometime? Stu.xXx.' It was those kisses that made me suspicious. I figured some of the other girls at work had guessed my feelings and were playing a cruel trick. So I just turned my phone off without replying and tried to sleep. The next shift I had, as well as not talking to

Stu, I also ignored pretty much everyone else there in the confusion of my suspicions about who had sent the message. All the same, that night I kept waking up and reaching for the fridge light of my mobile to binge on the sweet hope still sitting in my inbox. I replied in the morning.

Why Stu ever thought to ask me out is a mystery. His continued invitations to the pub, cinema, zoo, picnics, no less of one. I was silent and blushing and awkward throughout. In the end, we settled for lying in each other's bedrooms listening to music, and the relief of other vocals plying the distance between our lips made me at last relax. We took a holiday together. Coming up off the beach he had me sit on the wall while he brushed the sand from my feet with his hands.

*　*　*

I don't know exactly where my words to him on the boat that afternoon came from. He had come by as normal and I was pretty cheerful about something, I remember. Maybe there'd been more customers than usual or some new books had been delivered. Whatever it was, I was making him tea and chattering and, in a pause I left, he asked how I was planning on covering the outgoings this month or should he be expecting to receive another tearful phone call begging him to tide things over until business picked up some more in spring. I start yelling. 'It's getting better,' I insist. 'Look at today.'

'You're deceiving yourself. The figures are worse than ever.'

'It's not your business any more. If things are crap, what's it to you?'

'Because I can't see you like this. I can't take it. You need to sort things out.'

'You need to GO AWAY! Go away from me. Leave. This is what I CHOSE. This is what I WANT.'

Two customers walk in then. I'm making those horrible sobbing gulps and Stu is just standing, face contorted, at the bottom of the front steps. The other couple know straight away they've walked in on something and talk loudly and brightly to each other to cover for us. There are no words for us now, though. There is nothing to string together any more.

He sends a text maybe half an hour later saying sorry; telling me to drive safe in all the snow. All I can think of is how, early on when we were dating, I once drove past him in his car coming up the lane to work. I was still looking at him in the rear mirror when I drove into a hedge. I felt stupid then. But

I was in love. I have never loved him more, never been more stupid, when I text back: 'This is too difficult. Let's not see each other for a while.xx.'

59

BUT

On Wednesdays at the school library I take a creative writing class. Mostly they write about death or One Direction, once even an astonishing haiku hybrid of the two. In today's we're looking at good first lines, so they've found their favourite books from the shelves and are seated around a table taking turns to read the openings aloud and discuss why they're effective. I'm only half listening, half watching a Year 11 boy on the field outside picking his nose in goal. It's April and, after a cold winter and late snow, the weather has finally turned. The girl who's next to read complains of the sun in her eyes so I get up to pull the blue window-blinds across and she begins: 'But I didn't want to go to grandma's! I hated going there.'

It is a good start, we all agree. 'What's so unusual about the first word?' I ask.

'It's normally in the middle of a sentence rather than the start?' one girl suggests timidly.

'Brilliant! It's called a conjunction — a part

of speech that connects two different ideas or clauses. So what's the effect of using it to begin a sentence?'

'We want to know what came before?'

'Absolutely.'

'And could we also use 'but' to end a sentence?' A Year 8 girl poses.

'Why not?' I say. 'It would leave us wanting to know what happened next.'

When the session's over I take my bike from the metal cages out the front and pedal home, one hand holding my bag down in the front basket when I cycle over the pot-holes by the bridge. My route takes me over the canal, not far from where the bookshop is moored, undergoing its toiletry transformation plus a few extra bits of refurbishment. On a whim, I detour to take a quick look. It has been stripped of all the books, shelves and other furniture for a new ceiling to be fitted and a fresh lick of paint. It's the first time I've seen the new colour scheme. No longer black and cream inside, I've chosen a dark grey for the area underneath the upper incline of the walls. Above it, and the ceiling too, is fresh white. The overall effect pleases me. I sit on the lip of the front door and take my phone out to tell Stu how great it looks. The envelope he sent last year falls out of the same pocket.

Today I waste no time opening it. The corners have creased and torn in my bag all these months and the seal flap no longer sticks down from being lifted so often. I know what it says but seeing the words on the lined paper, the black surety of them, is always better. The paper is folded twice lengthways and twice across. On the first flap is an RSVP address, which opens to a sentence I recognised even then: 'Been thinking about this for a while, but do you want to go for a drink sometime?'

Inside, typewritten, are all the words we used to borrow from songs in those early, quiet, laying down days. There are snatches of band lyrics and the borrowed phrasings of singer songwriters. There is everyone from Mike Skinner to Karen Carpenter, Beck, Maximo Park, Foreigner, The Flaming Lips, and more, and still more. So strangely populated, this page. It says at the top: 'This ain't a love song.' At the end: It is not signed. It is from a Prince of Discs.

I fold it up again, this time placing his text question first. That has the only word we needed and the one we never will again: that conjunction, that joining word. I wrote back then, I say it still now: Yes. Yes. There is no 'but'.

60

THE BOOKSHOP THAT
FLOATED AWAY

15th October 2011, Saltaire, Yorkshire

It was here yesterday; black and cream and narrow, with the slouched backs of pizza crusts left over on the floor inside and book spines skirting every wall. There were plastic cups uncleared on the bench, bruised suns of wine eclipsed beneath them. Bottles emptied long shadows against a radiator. On the desk a paperback had tented its chapters under the glow of the lamp.

'It was here yesterday.' I try to sound confident, but my head, still full with last night's drink, is leaking self-doubt around the sides of my tongue and it makes my words smudge together.

'It was here yesterday,' James concedes, hiding his disgust behind a mask of polite bafflement. Charlotte, his daughter, is Cossack dancing along the towpath in her Saturday football kit. She has been squatting repeatedly like this since we got out the car and discovered the bookshop had floated away.

When they go I have to sit down for a while on a bench. James has promised to come back once he's delivered Charlotte to her match. I am full of assurances that it can't be far away. It's sixty foot long. It's very heavy. It's a *bookshop*, I reason. I am full of hope and stale breath to them. But, sitting on the bench after, gloom takes hold and I presume the boat is sunk or stolen or has been torched. In the space where it was, a shoal of autumn leaves sun and wait.

After a few minutes the possibility that I moved the boat myself starts giving some comfort. It is plausible. The albatross of vodka tonics and cheap Zinfandel hung over my head this morning suggests I am likely to blame. There was a book club and a weight of alcohol and why not requests for a boozy cruise too? It is simply a case of strolling down the towpath to find where I moored it. If not that, then perhaps I left the doors unlocked — wide open even — and some teenagers are recouping an anti-climactic 4mph joyride by sniffing glue on the gunwales. Either way, I must get up and walk. The surprise of being able to do this briefly clears my head. There is an indignation of geese by the bridge but they move and after that it gets easier.

As I walk, the horror of the morning lifts slightly. I woke up in a strange room in an unfamiliar house. Overnight it seemed that my limbs had grown and no longer fitted the bed. My feet hung through a gap in the wooden frame into space, and only when I sat up did it become apparent why; I was on the top of a child's bunk. More disconcerting was a girl's face at the summit of the ladder. She had brown hair and was wearing glasses and pink pyjamas. I couldn't recall having ever met her before, although she seemed to know a lot about me. 'Good, you're awake at last. I've made a canal boat on the carpet. Would you like to play in it, Sarah?' I was too scared to refuse.

It struck me then, standing at an imaginary tiller and about to embark on an ambitious voyage of a small child's creation, that I had died and passed to the afterlife. That the spirit world was a ten-year-old's bedroom came as no real surprise. It was my just desserts for years of refusing to grow up. What did take me aback was the smell of toast wafting through the door and, five minutes later, the appearance of a woman called Sam who once, a long time ago last night, had been on my boat leading a book club called Reading Between the Wines. 'So you've met my daughter Charlotte,' she smiles kindly.

344

I don't have to walk far before I find the boat. The relief makes me sway and then throw up into a hedge. I wipe my mouth with a tissue and then stagger gratefully up the towpath towards my bookshop. It rests in the middle of the canal, equidistant from both sides, with its ropes hanging into the water bow and stern. It does not move one inch, as if the trailing lines alone are anchoring it to the spot. There is no way I can reach it until it drifts nearer to my side or to the far bank. I reach for the ground and sit down, cross-legged, waiting for either of these outcomes.

An old man walks up the towpath a quarter of an hour later. He stops and stands close to me, following my gaze to the boat. 'Is that yours, girl?' he asks. I nod and smile. 'You'll be here a long time, I think. That water's not moving anywhere.' Again, I nod. We both watch it in silence for some minutes before he starts cackling to himself. After he's collected his mirth he turns to me, straight-faced, and says: 'You know what you need to pass the time, eh?' I shake my head, my forehead gathered into a frown against the sun. 'You need a good book,' he says, chuckling hard again and reluctantly turning to go. I hear him say it again and again to himself as he walks away — A good book! A good book!

She needs a good book! — and his laughter rustling with the leaves.

I don't though. Not now, I don't. I will watch my boat until it comes to me, I'll wait however long that takes. The morning ticks back and forth between the two mills pressing over us, and a peculiar clarity works on me there. Through the shop window I can make out, on the inside wall, the business strap line pilfered from the end of *The Great Gatsby*, a book I once believed to be perfect. I am wrong about many things, but this mistake, this makes me smile. It's the bit about always having to fight the flow, always being taken back. I used to think that the best closing line of any book. Now I'm not so sure how true it is. Looking at the unmoved bookshop, I can't see which way the current will take it. My sister was right all along, you can't see anything under there. It might be a thing of a bygone age; or maybe there's something quietly carrying it forward. You can't see anything under there. Once there were even two birds.

So there's a better ending, but only Time, that queer parent, will tell. I stand up to catch the shadow cast by the tiller bar on the water. It looks like a clock hand striking the hour. Or, when I squint, like a wand.

346

Acknowledgements
(aka THE PRAISE BE!
POCKET BOOK)

I am grateful for:

1. Avocado.
2. Beautiful babies.
3. Cats.
4. The Acquisitor being occasionally lost for words.
5. Ears to listen to ~~The Acquisitor's online videos~~ Kate Bush singing 'Running Up That Hill'.
6. FUDs. Although the love waned when I realised squatting behind hedgerow is less faff.
7. Graeme — you owe me a tattoo . . .
8. Hugh and all at Constable & Robinson.
9. Independent booksellers, brothers in arms.
10. Jed — I believe in sea monsters now.
11. Kind strangers of the UK who fed, clothed, trimmed, washed, watered, mattressed, advised, shod, liquored, encouraged and — most importantly — befriended me. You bought books, you swapped books,

you saw me under swing bridges and through locks and around the entire country. I can't thank you enough.

12. Lee Rourke's *The Canal*.
13. Mr Johnson.
14. Nicholson's *Waterways Guides* — I'd be lost without you.
15. Obviously there are too many pubs to mention individually but, for being so sensitive to my bursting bladder at 9 a.m. one Sunday morning, The Dog and Doublet on the Birmingham & Fazeley locks.
16. Parents — you have accommodated *this* book and *that* boat in every way possible. I love you.
17. Quiet hours undisturbed by HSBC call centres.
18. Rebecca — my first shipmate, my ultimate captain. Let's take a voyage on the HMS Bunk Ladder again soon.
19. Scurvy lads.
20. ~~The Complete Guide to Starting and Running a Bookshop~~ *How to be Idle/ How to be Free*.
21. Unhealthily large servings of lasagne — I missed you baby.
22. Vann, David — for a helpful perspective on debt.
23. Wellcome Trust's delectably warm showers and tasty breakfast buffet — and my

wonderful sister-in-law Christy for the introduction.

24. XL hooded jumpers — you fit over fifteen layers of clothing like a glove. You hide my greasy locks.
25. Yorkshire Tea.
26. Zero VAT on books.
27. Twitter. Social media, I was wrong about you.
28. *Maidens' Trip* by Emma Smith.
29. Paul — you ate all my biscuits, you drove me to Paris. I guess the balance works out in your favour.
30. British Waterways — you were all angels in blue branded T-shirts.
31. Barry, Simon, George and all at Barton Marina, where this bookshop was born.
32. The little boy in Nottingham who made my heart sing when he heralded The Book Barge 'the most unexpected thing in the universe'. Damn right it is!
33. Bristol Harbour master — let bygone rules be bygones.
34. Bristol pals and Bristol crew. You answered the call. Your city is proud and Joseph is too.
35. BBC Bristol — thanks for the publicity!
36. Victoria sponge — truly, a cake of distinction.
37. The improbable cork-screwing talent of

the humble Allen key.

38. Rob Isaacs — when I was broke, you gave me gainful employment and your flat.

39. Anna Sewell — and my sister Clare for once, long ago, lending me her *Black Beauty* book and tape set.

40. Nelson — RIP admiral lord of the flies.

41. Napoleon Bunnyparte — my lucky rabbit's foot.

42. All those beautiful horses . . .

43. All those taciturn herons . . .

44. Friends who helped me in more ways than they'll ever know — Ali, Katie, Laura, Helena, Twinny, Fran, Kate, Chris, Graham, Emily and Helen.

45. Jamie — for your love and kindness when it was most needed.

46. www.canalplan.org.uk

47. Helen, Andy and www.wildsidepreserves-.co.uk

48. www.clothingforcorrespondence.com

49. www.denstore.bigcartel.com

50. www.tommedwell.com

51. Amazon — when you don't pay taxes you make me look gooooood.

52. Lock keepers — few and far between, but guaranteed satisfaction.

53. James, Sam, Charlotte and Bin Weevils — thanks for making me feel one of the family.

54. JD Narrowboats — you crafted a fine vessel in Joseph.

55. James Brindley: 'He knew Water, its Weight and Strength, / Turn'd Brooks, made Soughs to a great Length; / While he used the Miner's Blast, / He stopp'd Currents from running too fast; / There ne'er was paid such Attention / As he did to Navigation.'

56. Any help offered with tax returns.

57. Black Books, for the succinct truth: 'The pay's not great, but the work is hard.'

58. Samuel Johnson, for *that* 'barge' definition.

59. Occasional custom.

60. Reaching the halfway point of this ridiculous challenge.

61. At least not having to write an acknowledgements page now . . .

62. The glass tending to be half full.

63. Six months, no frostbite!

64. Six months, no cirrhosis!

65. The Acquisitor not being around in tsarist Russia — Peter the 'Grateful' doesn't quite have the same ring . . .

66. Four plump pillows to prop me up in bed while I churned this book out.

67. The incongruous statue of Captain Edward Smith in Lichfield's Beacon Park, 'bequeathing to his countrymen the memory

and example of a great heart'.

68. Never having worn a windlass holster.
69. Clean fingernails — finally — eighteen months on.
70. Chekhov — for getting it (and getting some! A recent Guardian article attests to some thirty-three lovers — and counting — before he died aged forty-four).
71. The mystery of the sleeping bag: What does it do with our socks?
72. Any opportunity for a lie-in.
73. Kings Place, York Way. Your disabled toilet + my ablutions = a happy, clean bookseller all day.
74. Libraries — fight on!
75. Pleasant surprises: sunshine in British summertime, the dentist saying I don't need a filling, the occasional longevity of pigeons.
76. George Whitman.
77. Black tights.
78. Animal rights.
79. Swans in flight.
80. Things that rhyme, right?
81. Cacti and other unneedy house plants.
82. Bread and butter pudding.
83. Sticky toffee pudding.
84. Custard.
85. Dessertification in all its calorific forms.
86. Play.

87. Pools.
88. People who buy in hardback.
89. The audacity of hope (Obama's words, not mine).
90. The shaky belief that I have imagination enough to fill this list with another thirty beneficences.
91. Jen Campbell, for extraordinary book-selling and championing my blog.
92. EL James's gift to the English literary canon . . .
93. . . . how easy some lies come.
94. The dream of French bookselling — still alive and kicking and a little hungry for macarons.
95. Claire Massey, Simon Savidge and all the other generous book bloggers of this world.
96. Six months, no Weil's Disease!
97. Six months, no falling down a weir!
98. The 4mph unravelling of my country.
99. Sponsorship, patronage or any other financial leg-ups from a willing party/large corporation/billionaire CEO/ Russian oligarch.My VIP curry card.
100. Naïveté.
101. The polite response from Red Bull who, following a request for sponsorship to take the boat to Paris, wrote back: *Thank you for contacting Red Bull, sponsors of*

some of the world's most extreme stunts and dangerous sports. Unfortunately, having reviewed your application, we cannot neatly fit narrow boating into the extreme stunt nor dangerous sport category. We wish you luck with your future canal endeavours.

102. My trusty butcher's bike . . .
103. . . . and my more feminine ladies shopper.
104. Southern Comfort.
105. The humble bookmark.
106. The handy credit card.
107. The kids and staff at Paget High School Library . . .
108. . . . the bell ringing for home time nonetheless.
109. Never having painted a rose nor a castle on any of my watering cans.
110. The Itinerant Poetry Librarian — a guerilla public lending service par excellence.
111. Book clubs, especially my own degenerate lot.
112. The Plimsoll line.
113. A chunky knit.
114. Narsh and crew — you're hired!
115. Anyone who's still reading this exhaustive (exhaust-*ing*?) list.
116. My boat — 'we are suspended in dread' (Heidegger).

117. My books — we live happily ever after.
118. Stuart — for your love, which *does* make me shed acquisi-tears, and for everything.
119. The end.

WHEN FRASER MET BILLY

Louise Booth

Fraser was an autistic three-year-old boy, prone to anxiety and sudden meltdowns over seemingly the most trivial things. Day-to-day life in the Booth household was difficult. To Fraser's parents, Louise and Chris, the future looked bleak. But then Fraser met Billy, a grey and white rescue cat, and the two formed an instant connection. As Billy remained by his side, providing calm, reassurance and affection, Fraser made remarkable advances in his confidence, social interactions and contentment. Their profound bond brightens the whole family's lives — and has brought them many hilarious and touching moments along the way.

MUM'S ARMY

Winifred Phillips and Shannon Kyle

During the Second World War, young trainee nurse Winifred Phillips confided to her RAF boyfriend George Wheeler that she rather liked the idea of joining the Army herself . . . Enlisting in the ATS in 1948, she embarked upon twenty-two years' service in that and the WRAC, travelling the globe and reaching the rank of Warrant Officer Class Two. From dodging NCOs whilst eating illicit fish and chips, to dispatching invading snakes — and ultimately becoming one of the first two women to be admitted to the Royal Hospital as Chelsea Pensioners — this is Philly's story.

LIFE BELOW STAIRS

Alison Maloney

Upstairs: a picture of elegance and calm, adorned with social gatherings and extravagantly envisioned dinner parties. Downstairs: a hive of domestic activity, supported by a body of staff painstakingly devoted to ensuring the smooth running of the household . . . Brimming with family secrets, society scandal and elaborate fashion, the world of the aristocratic Edwardian household has captured the minds of millions of modern people. But what was it like for those who really kept such a household running? From pay and regulations, to perks and entertainment — and even romance — the minutiae of servants' lives provide a fascinating glimpse into their below-stairs world.

A CONVERSATION ABOUT HAPPINESS

Mikey Cuddihy

When Mikey Cuddihy was orphaned at the age of nine, her life exploded. She was sent from New York to board at the experimental Summerhill School in Suffolk, and abandoned there. The setting was apparently idyllic: lessons were optional, pupils made the rules, and the late sixties were in full swing. But with this total freedom came danger . . . Mikey navigated this strange world of permissiveness and neglect, forging an identity almost in defiance of it. *A Conversation About Happiness* is a vivid and intense memoir of coming of age amidst the unravelling social experiment of sixties and seventies Britain.